ו אברהם בן הרמב"ם

...רשות ועל האגדות

Understanding *Ḥ*a*Z*a"L

being a chapter from

KIFĀYAT AL-ʿĀBIDĪN (HAMASPIQ LEỌVDE HASHEM)

or

A COMPREHENSIVE GUIDE FOR THE SERVANTS OF GOD

by

Avraham ben HaRaMBa"M

◆ ◆ ◆

translated and annotated by

RABBI YITZHAK BERDUGO

Understanding Ḥaza"L

First Edition, 2022

ISBN:

Paperback: 9798362152260

Hardback: 9798362590741

www.daat.press

דפוס דעת

DA'AT PRESS

DA'AT PRESS

עיצוב, דפוס, ועריכה ע"י אבנר ישורון
design, typesetting, and editing by Avner Yeshurun
ayeshurun@gmail.com / +1 (305)-761-3561
Miami Beach, FL
2022

◆

editing by Nachman Davies

Rabbi Yitzhak Berdugo can be reached at isaaczb@gmail.com

Contents

הסכמות / Rabbinic Approbations ix

Translator's Foreword xxii
Rabbi Yitzhak Berdugo

Translator's Preface xxxii
Links between the Geonim and the Sepharadim

Editor's Preface liv
The sphere of conviction

Chapter 1: Introduction 60
The need for proper guidance in the study of midrashic and aggadic passages

Chapter 2 68
Conviction and proper perception in matters of aggadah

Chapter 3 104
The five categories of exegesis

Chapter 4 124
The four types of narratives

Chapter 5 156
Narratives and exegeses assembled from multiple components

Chapter 6 162
Conclusion

Contributors clxx

About Da'at Press clxxiii

◆ ◆ ◆

הסכמות / Rabbinic Approbations

I saw and studied the book which yields lovely fawns,[1] the work of the great and esteemed man, the distinguished scholar, illustrious in Torah and in the pure awe of Heaven, the learned rabbi, the stronghold and tower, who constantly busies himself with Torah, who is astute and understanding, may his Rock and Redeemer preserve him, Rabbi Yitzhak Berdugo, may he live good and lengthy days.

The book is a commentary on an essay from *HaMaspiq LeOvde HaShem* by Rabbenu Avraham ben HaRaMBa"M, of blessed memory. Rabbi Berdugo has done everything in good sense and with knowledge,[2] and I wish to bless him that the will of God be fulfilled through him,[3] and that he may bring to light Torah in its glory, ordered in all and secured,[4] in good health and good light, and may his name be like the names of the great ones in the land,[5] Amen, may His will be such.

Rabbi Eliyahu Abergel
Chief Judge of Rabbinical Courts
Jerusalem

---

[1] based on Genesis 49:21
[2] based on Psalms 119:66
[3] based on Isaiah 53:10
[4] based on II Samuel 23:5
[5] based on II Samuel 7:9

Rabbi Eliyahu Abergel
Chief Judge of Rabbinical Courts
Jerusalem
& Rabbi Of Bak'ah Neighborhood in Jerusalem
& Chief Rabbi of "Tzoof Devash" Yeshiva

הרב אליהו אבירז'ל
ראש אבות בתי הדין הרבניים
ירושלים
רב שכונת בקעה, וראש ישיבת צוף דב"ש
מחבר שו"ת דברות אליהו י"ב חלקים

ב"ה [illegible]

הסכמה..

ראיתי ועיינתי בספר, בנידון אמרי שפר, מעשה ידיו
של האי גברא רבה ויקירא החכם השלם המופלג בתורה ויר"ש
הרה"ג מלונו. דעסיק באורייתא תדירא. משכיל ונבון וכו'
הרב יצחק הכהן שליט"א הספר הוא פירוש על מאמרים
מספרו המספיק לעובדי ה'. של רבינו אברהם בן הרמב"ם זצ"ל
עשה הכל בטוב טעם ודעת. והנני לברכו שחפץ
ה' בידו יצליח להוציא לאורה תורה מבוארה,
ערוכה בכל ושמורה. בבריאות טובה ונהורא מעליא
ויהיה שמו כשם הגדולים אשר בארץ אכי"ר

אליהו אבירזיל

הרב אליהו אבירזיל * ראב"ד * אבות בתי הדין הרבניים * ירושלים

Address: 21 Dan Street, Jerusalem
Tel: 02-6724822 Fax: 02-6727369 Israel

מעונו: רח' דן 21 שכונת בקעה, ירושלים
טל: 02-6724822 פקס: 02-6727369 ישראל

28/01/2011 11:47 +972-26727369 HARAV ABERGEL PAGE 01/01

In honor of my dear friend, the esteemed and great Rabbi, Rabbi Yitzhak Berdugo,

I was delighted and filled with joy upon seeing the wonderful work you have accomplished in translating the work of *Understanding the Derashot & Aggadot of Hazal* by our teacher and master Rabbi Avraham ben Rambam, a section from his magnum opus, *Hamaspiq LeOvdei Hashem.*

This book is crucial book in order to educate oneself in learning the *aggadot* of our Sages in the correct manner. It is known that the RaMBa"M wrote in his preface to his *Perush HaMishnah* that there is a great benefit in studying the *aggadot* of our Sages, for they contain within them the Torah's profound and remarkable secrets.

I trust in you, as a teacher with distinguished students (whom I have met), that no stumbling block will come from you. Be strong and courageous. May it be the will of God that your fountains be disseminated abroad and that you will be able to increase the Torah and its glory, and that we will see you amongst the greatest of the world.

Regards,

Rabbi Eliyahu Ben Haim

Av Bet Din, Mekor Haim , New York

Rabbinical Court | **בית דין צדק**

New York | ניו יורק

147-02 76th Road Flushing NY 11367 347-415-5681

Rabbi Eliyahu Ben-Chaim, Chairman

בס״ד
תמוז תשפ״ב

לכבוד ידידי היקר הרב הגדול לעוז ומגדול הרב יצחק בירדוגו

שמחתי ויגל לבי על העבודה הנפלאה שעשית לתרגם את המאמר על הדרשות ועל האגדות מאת רבינו אברהם בן הרמב״ם מתוך ספר המספיק לעובדי השם. וזה ספר חשוב מאד לפתוח את העיניים על למוד אגדות חז״ל בדרך הנכונה. וידוע שהרמב״ם כתב (בהקדמה לפירוש המשניות) שיש תועלת גדולה בלימוד אגדות חז״ל, דיש בהם סתרי תורה עמוקים ונפלאים.

ובטוחני בך וגם כראש כולל עם תלמידים חשובים כפי שהכרתי שלא תצא תקלה מתחת ידך. חזק ואמץ, יהי רצון שיפוצו מעינותיך חוצה ותזכה להגדיל תורה ולהאדירה, ונראה אותך כאחד הגדולים בארץ.

אליהו בן חיים

נאם : הרב אליהו בן חיים

Rabbi Eliyahu Ben Haim Av Beit Din NY

בס"ד

ROHR TALMUDIC UNIVERSITY CAMPUS

ישיבה וכולל בית משה חיים

TALMUDIC UNIVERSITY

HaRav Yochanan Zweig, shlita
Rosh HaYeshiva

Rabbi Yitzchak Zweig
President

16th Tammuz 5782

Lichvod R' Yitzhak Berdugo,

I have the privilege of calling R' Yitzhak a Talmid. From the moment he joined the Yeshiva, I knew he was special and unique. He is an outstandingly devoted Talmid Chachum who truly understands how to learn. Furthermore, I've witnessed him being as devoted to ensuring those around him have the tools to properly learn and understand the text as it's meant to be read.

It is a real honor for the Shul of Baal Harbour to have Rabbi Berdugo as their Rosh Kollel. He has continued the Berdugo family's legacy of generations of Torah Scholars. I would highly recommend this Sefer as a worthwhile read, his erudition clearly is evident. One can rely on R' Yitzhak's Psak Halacha as he is an expert in both Sephardic and Ashkanaz law - derived from the teachings of the Rosh.

May the Ribono Shel Olem continue to give him the strength to inspire and educate the future Doros of Klal Yisroel for many years to come with Arichas Yamim for him and his family.

With much admiration,

Rabbi Yochanan Zweig

4000 Alton Road
Miami Beach, FL 33140

Tel: (305) 534-7050
Fax: (305) 534-8444

ALFRED AND SADYE SWIRE COLLEGE OF JUDAIC STUDIES

www.talmudicu.edu

בס"ד

ישיבה וכולל בית משה חיים

TALMUDIC UNIVERSITY

ROHR TALMUDIC UNIVERSITY CAMPUS

HaRav Yochanan Zweig, shlita
Rosh HaYeshiva

Rabbi Yitzchak Zweig
President

לכבוד הרה״ג יצחק בירדוגו,

זכות הוא לי לכנות את הרב יצחק 'תלמיד'. מהרגע שהצטרף לישיבתינו ידעתי שהינו מיוחד במינו ולגדולות נוצר. הנ״ל הוא תלמיד חכם מופלג שמבין היטב לימוד תורה מהו, ואיך ללומדו. בנוסף, אני יכול להעיד על ההשקעה והמאמץ שהנ״ל דואג לסובבים אותו, ובפרט לתלמידיו, שיהיה להם את הכלים הנכונים כדי שיוכלו ללמוד בדרך הישרה והנכונה, ולהבין את הכתוב כדבעי.

זכות הוא לבית הכנסת הגדול שבבאל הארבור, שתלמידי הרה״ג יצחק, עומד בראשות הכולל שם ויהיה להם למגדל אור תורני. מגזע אראלים ותרשישים, הרה״ג יצחק ממשיך את נצר מפשחת ברדוגו ונושא את הלפיד המשפחתי בגאון ועוז שלא תכבה. הנני ממליץ בחום על הספר שבידכם, שהינו מרתק ביותר, ובפרט שבהירותו והסברתו נראים לעין כל. אפשר לסמוך על כח הפסק של הרה״ג יצחק שהינו מומחה גדול בהלכה הן לבני ספרד והן לבני אשכנז (ההולכים לרוב אחר רבינו הרא״ש).

יה״ר מלפני אבינו שבשמים שיעניק לו ולכל משפחתו את הכח ויכולת להשפיע וללמד את המשך הדור של עם ישראל עד זקנה ושיבה.

בכבוד רב,

הרב יוחנן משה צווייג

4000 Alton Road
Miami Beach, FL 33140

Tel: (305) 534-7050
Fax: (305) 534-8444

ALFRED AND SADYE SWIRE COLLEGE OF JUDAIC STUDIES

www.talmudicu.edu

the S&PHARDI community ק״ק שער השמים

בית דין דק״ק ספרדים לונדון והמדינה
Sephardi Beth Din

בס"ד

In honor of my dear friend, Rabbi Yitzhak Berdugo SHeLIṬ"A

My heart rejoiced and my soul was enlightened when I saw the new English translation of Rabbenu Avraham ben HaRaMBa"M's work on *Understanding the Derashot & Aggadot of Hazal*. This work is unparalleled in shedding light on the approach of Rabbenu Avraham and his father, and is especially important considering the developments of science in our time and the religious friction that constantly arises. The translation is written in a clear and eloquent manner, with crucial footnotes that refer to additional sources, in particular to the Rambam's writings. These notes shed light on Rabbenu Avraham's approach and loyalty to his father's path throughout the work.

I personally know Rabbi Yitzhak as a relentless scholar who constantly labors in the realms of Torah. Possessing both a broad and in-depth understanding of Torah, I am sure that the translation of this work will serve as an opening to many towards the Torah of our Rabbi (Rabbenu Avraham), and in particular to the important topics that this work deals with.

I concur with the other approbations given to Rabbi Yitzhak and bless that his fountains will be spread abroad and that he will bring the hearts of Israel closer to their Father in Heaven and His Torah.

Regards,

Dayan Ofer Livnat,

Teacher at Kollel Eretz Hemdah, Jerusalem & *Dayan* at the Sephardi Bet Din, London.

Sephardi Beth Din

The S&P Sephardi Community
119-121 Brent Street, London, NW4 2DX
T 020 7289 2573

www.sephardi.org.uk

The home of the Sephardi community since 1656

the S&PHARDI community ק״ק שער השמים

בית דין דק״ק ספרדים לונדון והמדינה
Sephardi Beth Din

בס"ד

לכבוד ידידי הרב יצחק בירדוגו שליט"א

שמח ליבי ותגל נפשי בראותי את התרגום החדש לאנגלית של המאמר על הדרשות ועל האגדות של רבי אברהם בן הרמב"ם, בנו של הנשר הגדול רבן של כל ישראל הרמב"ם זצ"ל. מאמר זה חשוב מאין כמותו להאיר את דרכו של רבי אברהם ואביו, ובפרט לאור ההתמודדות האמונית עם התפתחויות המדע בימינו. התרגום כתוב בצורה ברורה וקולחת, עם הערות שוליים חשובות מאוד המפנות למקורות נוספים ובפרט לכתבי הרמב"ם, שיש בהם להאיר את דרכו של רבי אברהם ונאמנותו לדרכו של אביו גם במאמר זה.
מכיר אני את הרב יצחק כמתמיד עצום השוקד על דלתות התורה בבקיאות רבה ובסברא עמוקה וישרה, ובטוח אני שהתרגום של החיבור הנ"ל יפתח פתח לרבים לתורתו של רבינו ובפרט בנושאים החשובים שהמאמר עוסק בהם.
מצטרף אני ליתר ההסכמות כיהודה ועוד לקרא, ונברך את המחבר שיפוצו מעיינותיו חוצה ויזכה לקרב את לבם של ישראל לאביהם שבשמים ותורתו.

בברכה
עופר לבנת
ר"מ בכולל ארץ חמדה בירושלים ודיין בבית הדין הספרדי בלונדון

Sephardi Beth Din

The S&P Sephardi Community
119-121 Brent Street, London, NW4 2DX
T 020 7289 2573

www.sephardi.org.uk

The home of the Sephardi community since 1656

The works of Rabbenu Avraham Ben HaRaMBa"M are especially important.

Rabbi Yitzhak Berdugo translated a portion into English in order to make it accessible to English readers. His translation is a very important contribution to spreading Rabbenu Avraham's views, which are essential to deciphering the *Aggadot* of our Sages, which are likened to *golden apples with silver plated vessels* (Proverbs 25:11).

Assuming that the translation is correct and accurate, I bless that there will be no mishap from his works, and for the tremendous merits of the public at large will be his merit, the reward for which is a good reward from God.

Rabbi Ratzon Arusi
Grand Rabbi of Kiryat Ono & member of Israel's Chief Rabbinate Council

לק"י

מכון מש"ה – לחקר משנת הרמב"ם

מיסודה של "הליכות עם ישראל"

רח' הרצל 71, ת"ד 911 קרית אונו טל' 03-5351119 פקס' 1533-5351119

halichot@zahav.net.il www.Net-Sah.org

הרב רצון ערוסי

רב העיר קרית אונו

חבר מועצת הרבנות הראשית לישראל

יו"ר הליכות עם ישראל

ונשיא מכון מש"ה

ו' באב תשפ"ב

3.8.22

הסכמה

שו"ת הראב"ם הוא חיבור חשוב מאוד.

הרב **יצחק ברדוגו** תרגמו לאנגלית כדי להנגישו לדוברי אנגלית. תרגומו הוא בבחינת תרומה חשובה למדי כדי להפיץ את רעיונותיו של הראב"ם, שהם מפתחות לפענוח אגדות חז"ל, שהן בגדר תפוחי זהב במשכיות כסף.

ככל שהתרגום נכון ומדויק, הנני מברכו שלא תצא תקלה מתחת ידיו, וזיכוי הרבים יעמוד לו כזכות, שהגמול לה הוא גמול טוב מה'.

בברכה

רצון ב"ר יוסף **ערוסי** הלוי

Translator's Foreword

Rabbi Yitzhak Berdugo

RABBENU AVRAHAM BEN HARAMBA"M

Rabbenu Avraham ben HaRaMBa"M, also known as RAVa"M, was born in the city of Fostat (ancient Cairo), Egypt, in 1186 CE, and passed away there in 1237 CE, at the age of fifty-two.

His mother, Jamila, HaRaMBa"M's second wife, was the daughter of R. Mishael Halevi. Rabbenu Avraham married the daughter of R. Ḥananel ben Shemuel[1]; she bore him two sons, R. David HaNagid[2] (who served as *Nagid* after his father), and R. Ọvadyah,[3] who was known for his piety. Rabbenu Avraham's brother-in-law (who married R. Ḥananel ben Shemuel's other daughter), with whom he had an extremely close relationship, was R. Peraḥya ben Nissim,[4] *Dayan* of Belbes (north-east of Cairo).[5]

Rabbenu Avraham, the only son of the illustrious RaMBa"M, was born to him during the peak of his fame, when HaRaMBa"M was fify-one years old. Writing to one of his closest disciples, Yoseph Ibn Ạqnin, HaRaMBa"M describes the considerable talent his son possesses, the joy he gives him, and the aspirations he has for him:

> Amongst all my affairs, I only take consolation in two things, (one) when I examine and analyse things, and (two) that God, may He be praised, gave my son Avraham charm and favour, which stems from the blessing of the one after whom he is named[6]...For he is modest

1 author of a commentary on the *RI"F* (*Ẹruvin, Qidushin*)

2 R. David ben Avraham HaNagid (1222–1300), author of *Midrash David*, a commentary on the Torah and tractate *Avot*. The name "David HaNagid" is also given to a later member of the Maimuni dynasty, R. David ben Joshua (d. circa 1414). Frequently, they are differentiated as David HaNagid I and David HaNagid II.

3 author of *Al-Maqala al-Hawardiyya* (*Ma'amar Habe'er – The Treatise of the Pool*)

4 author of a commentary on the *RI"F* (*Shabbat*)

5 as can been seen in letters from the Cairo Geniza

6 meaning: Avraham the Patriarch

> and humble amongst the people. Along with these good qualities, he has a fine mind and a beautiful nature. He will have a name amongst the great ones, with the help of God, without a doubt. I ask from God, may He be praised, that He should watch over him, and place His grace over him.[1]

Rabbenu Avraham was raised under the close personal tuition of his father, and therefore directly received his father's wisdom in both Torah and the sciences. Many matters which HaRaMBa"M did not include in his works were transmitted solely to Rabbenu Avraham.

Near the end of his life, HaRaMBa"M fell ill for about one year and remained weak even following his recovery from the acute stages of his illness, being bed-ridden for most of the day. At the age of sixty-seven, HaRaMBa"M passed away (1205 CE), when Rabbenu Avraham was only nineteen.

At this tender age he was appointed *Ra'is al-Yahud* (Leader of the Jews) of Egypt (though he did not receive the honorific title of *Nagid* until 1213), and thereafter he laboured to confirm and develop his father's legacy with competence and authority. Due to his immense talent, and following the prime educational years that he had spent with his father, Rabbenu Avraham proved to be the defender of the tradition and approach that he had directly received. He held this position for thirty-three years, and bequeathed it to his family for five consecutive generations.

As *Nagid*, it was his responsibility to appoint *Dayanim* in Egypt; every court in the country turned to him for instruction and guidance. In their documents, following a statement of their court's location, the judges would add the approbation: "With the permission of our master, our great leader, Rabbi Avraham."

As a trained physician, he wrote medical works, and was even appointed personal physician of the Ayyubid sultan (Al-Kahmal). He also managed the Cairo Hospital alongside the famous Arab physician

1 *Igerot HaRaMBa"M, Teshuvat She'elot*, 71

and author, Ibn Abi Usaybi'a, who describes Rabbenu Avraham as follows:[1]

> He is tall and lean, and has an extremely sharp mind. He has a pleasant demeanour and manifests a good temper. He is an exceptional doctor and knowledgeable in the wisdom of medicine.

Due to his responsibilities in caring for the community and in managing the hospital, a heavy burden was placed on Rabbenu Avraham. Toward the end of a letter to R. Daniel the Babylonian, he describes his state of affairs:[2]

> Our time is consumed and busy with work for the gentiles, which we do not have the ability to evade, for if it were dependent on our choice, we would discard [such tasks and commitments] and not seek them, as the wise one said: "But the vine replied, 'Have I stopped yielding my new wine, which gladdens God and men, that I should go and wave above the trees?'"[3]

Many of the great scholars of his generation made it their duty to visit Rabbenu Avraham and take his counsel. When a number of the *Ba'ale Tosafot* of France journeyed to *Ereṣ Yisrael* in 1210 CE, they passed through Egypt to meet the young Rabbenu Avraham, who at the time was only twenty-five years of age.[4]

During his dynamic period of leadership, Rabbenu Avraham enacted many practices designed to revitalise the spiritual state of the Jewish people and guide the members of his own private, pietist, and ascetic community along the "special" path of devotion and contemplation described in his *Kifaya*. For example, he strove to renew the rituals of prostration and kneeling during certain prayers:[5] "One who

1 *Uyun al-Anba fi Tabaqat al-Attiba* (*History of Physicians*), ed. August Mueller, Cairo, 1882, p. 118

2 *History of Avraham son of RaMBa"M*, R. Reuven Margaliot, p. 28

3 Judges 9:13

4 *History of Avraham son of RaMBa"M*, R. Reuven Margaliot, page 18

5 While others objected to this renewal since it was a form of worship that the gentiles practiced, Rabbenu Avraham argued that a ritual does not become illegitimate merely because other religions adopt it (see N. Dana, *Sefer HaMaspiq LeOvde*

increases acts of kneeling and prostration is praiseworthy, for that is truly [a way to] serve God..."

He promoted the washing of one's hands and feet before prayer and before entering a synagogue,[1] as well as the practice of praying in orderly rows during congregational worship. However, when he felt certain customs were not to be followed, he would not hesitate to voice his opinion. He famously abolished the traditional custom whereby dignitaries of the community sat facing the congregation, with their backs towards the *Aron HaQodesh*, as he saw in it a disregard for the honour of the Torah:

> It is incorrect to sit other than facing the Holy (*Aron HaQodesh*) except for the elders who sit at the front of the synagogue. These elders are wise ones, based on the Sages' explanation of the verse "And you shall show deference to an elder"[2] they comment "An elder is one who acquired knowledge."[3] The reason why elders are permitted to sit in such a way is so that "the people should fear and respect them." In my mind, [their sitting this way] is not to be seen as obligatory, but rather as an allowance. Or possibly, the "elders," to whom the *Tanaim* of that generation were referring, were those with faces that evoked a greater [devotional] concen-

HaShem, Kitab Kifāyat al-ʿĀbidīn, II, chapter 25). Even when adapting Islamic Sufi practices, Rabbenu Avraham writes:

> Do not hold us in contempt for comparing [our] situation with that of the Sufis [of Islam], for it was the Sufis who imitated the [Hebrew] prophets and walked in their footsteps, not the prophets in theirs. (S.Rosenblatt, *Highways to Perfection*, II, Johns Hopkins Press, Baltimore 1938, p.320)

1 Ritual ablution had been central in temple worship and Rabbenu Avraham felt that its significance had been transferred to the congregational worship of the synagogue. (see *Kifaya*, ed. Dana, p. 69 and p. 184), but his pietist followers also received certain dispensations to pray the services privately at home in a personal *maqom qavua* from time to time for the sake of contemplative devotion. (see *Kifaya*, ed. Dana, p. 106 and p. 113). His father had insisted on ablution of "face, hands, and feet" before the morning prayers (*Mishneh Torah, Hilkhot Tefila* 4:3) but Rabbenu Avraham extended ablutions to all acts of prayer throughout the day. (see *Kifaya*, ed. Dana, p. 70).

2 Leviticus 19:32

3 *Qidushin* 32b

> tration on the part of the public, thus bringing them great benefit. [However], in our generation, such people or any coming close to their status are non-existent and no benefit will stem from contemporary elders sitting that way, "with their back to the Holy," other than their striving for power. Learning from them, causes people to sin rather than fulfill the purpose of their sitting, as described in the *Tosefta*. As we can see, in their sitting [facing the people] they are perceived as a group that is conversing amongst themselves rather than talking to God.[1]

Rabbenu Avraham defended his father's teachings both during his father's lifetime and even more so after his death. When there was no one left to respond to criticism or to settle seeming contradictions, Rabbenu Avraham clarified matters. Questions were sent to him from all over the world, as if he were HaRaMBa"M himself. When questions on the *Mishneh Torah* or *Sefer HaMiṣvot* occurred to R. Daniel the Babylonian, dean of the Baghdad *yeshiva* and a disciple of R. Samuel ben Ali, he would address them directly to Rabbenu Avraham for answering.[2]

Upon the translation of the the *Guide for the Perplexed* into Hebrew, controversy erupted across the globe. In defense of his father and the *Guide*, Rabbenu Avraham authored a work titled *Milḥamot HaShem*, the purpose of which was to eliminate any desecration of God's name due to the controversy.[3]

---

1 N. Dana, *Sefer HaMaspiq LeOvde HaShem, Kitab Kifāyat al-'Ābidīn*, p. 98

2 R. Daniel asked forty-seven questions, attempting to show that HaRaMBa"M had contradicted himself. Rabbenu Avraham answered each question individually in the work *Birkat Avraham*.

3 After studying Rabbenu Avraham's works, one can only ponder in astonishment at the displeasing and deceitful description given by the historian Heinrich Graetz:

> Abraham Maimuni was a man of learning, not of original, intellectual power. He followed with slavish fidelity in the footsteps of his great father, and appropriated his method of thought, surrendering his own intellectual independence. Abraham made the Maimunist system of teaching his own. Hence it happens, that what is striking originality in the father, appears in the son as a copy and an insignificant commonplace. Abraham Maimuni, it is true, enjoyed wide-spread esteem, but he was by no means an authority compelling attention and claiming submission.

HIS WORKS

During the fifty-two years of his life, Rabbenu Avraham authored a plethora of Jewish works, including commentaries on the Torah and halakhic responsa, as well as philosophical and ethical works. In addition to the countless texts which were written specifically to defend the ideas and works of his father, Rabbenu Avraham also authored works of great and original creativity which expounded upon his own ideas and reforms.

The following is a brief list of those works of Rabbenu Avraham which have been discovered (in whole or in part) to date:

- ***A Guide for the Servants of God (HaMaspiq LeỌvde HaShem - Kitab Kifāyat al-'Ābidīn):*** His magnum opus, composed in Judeo-Arabic. It deals with *Halakha*, piety and philosophy. Although only sparse fragments of the original work have survived, it is speculated that it was originally three times as long as his father's *Guide for the Perplexed*.[1]
- ***Commentary on the Torah (Perush HaTorah):*** only the commentaries on Genesis and Exodus remain extant.
- ***Responsa***
- ***Commentary on the Talmud (Diqduq Perush HaTalmud):*** a commentary to the tractate *Berakhot* and other tractates.
- ***Commentary on the Mishneh Torah (HaBiur Le' Iqre HaḤibur)***
- ***Treatise in Defence of the Pietists (Rasala):*** a short work or essay which he subtitled *An Enquiry into the Obligatory Character of Asceticism and its Recommendable Status in Religion.*
- ***The Special Book (HaSefer HaMeyuḥad)***[2]
- ***A Crown of Those who Know (Ạṭeret HaYode'im - Ta Al-Arafin)***
- ***Medical Works***
- ***The Blessing of Avraham (Birkat Avraham):*** answers to questions on and objections to the *Mishneh Torah* raised by R. Daniel the Babylonian.
- ***Miraculous Acts (Ma'ạse Nisim):*** answers to objections raised to *Sefer HaMiṣvot.*
- ***The Wars of God (Milḥamot HaShem):*** answers to objections raised regarding the *Guide for the Perplexed.*

---

1 As Professor Paul B. Fenton writes:

> By dint of its sheer volume, this work was probably the most important product of all Judaeo-Arabic literature. In its original form the work consisted of four parts, each divided into ten sections, each of which was again subdivided into ten chapters. Only two parts have come down to us in a more or less complete state, they alone containing 500 pages. Supposing that the remaining chapters were of the same scale, the work must have consisted of about 2,500 pages, i.e. thrice the size of the Mishneh Tôrâh. (Paul B.Fenton, *Maimonides—Father and Son: Continuity and Change*, in *Traditions of Maimonideanism*, ed. Fraenkel, Brill, Leiden, 2009, p. 115)

2 Only the names of this book and the next are known to us, not their content.

THIS WORK

This important and foundational work, *Ma'amar Al HaDerashot ve'al Ha'Aggadot*, is dedicated to clarifying the proper approach to understanding *midrashim* (exegeses) and *aggadot* (narratives) of our Sages according to the Geonic/Andalusian approach. Though examples of this approach can be found throughout the various works of his father and in the works of the *Rishonim* and *Geonim*, this is, perhaps, the first major work to examine the subject systematically and in detail.

At the beginning of this work, we are informed that Rabbenu Avraham is furthering his father's dream to compile a work explaining the various *midrashim* and *aggadot* of our Sages. Though HaRaMBa"M later reconsidered this project and decided to refrain from explaining the more difficult *midrashim*,[1] Rabbenu Avraham nevertheless felt it important to compile a work giving students the main principles for the systematic categorisation of various *midrashim* and *aggadot*.

This entire book is only one chapter from his magnum opus — *HaMaspiq LeOvde HaShem* — as can be seen in the notes to this translation[2] as well as in other chapters of his monumental work.[3] Only fragments of the original Judaeo-Arabic text, first completed in 1230 CE, remain. A significant citation of this chapter appears in a *Sefer* titled *Kevod Elohim*,[4] under the name "Explaining the Ways of *Midrashim* & *Aggadot*" (*Bi'ur Derekh HaMidrashim VeHaAggadot*). R. Ibn Migash mentions that he translated it into Hebrew at another's request.[5] Whereas R.

1 For HaRaMBa"M's full explanation, see chapter 1, footnote 6.

2 See chapter 1. (For further proofs, see Rabbi Professor Elazar Hurvits, *Sefer HaYovel In Honor of Dr. Joshua Finkel*, 1973, pp. 139-168)

3 See *Sefer HaMaspiq LeOvde HaShem, Kitab Kifāyat al-ʿĀbidīn*, ed. and trans. N. Dana, p. 316, Bar Ilan University, 1989, where Rabbenu Avraham writes:

> We already mentioned in the first section of this book [regarding how] the Sages utilised exaggerated expressions in narratives. And their statement "the Torah spoke employing exaggerated language, the prophets spoke employing exaggerated language, and the Sages spoke employing exaggerated language." (*Tamid* 29a)

4 Avraham Ibn Migash, Constantinople, 1586, p. 71

5 R. Avraham Ibn Migash also states that it was part of *HaMaspiq LeOvde Hashem*, and

Ibn Migash's translation was only completed in the late sixteenth century, we know of two earlier translations, the Oxford[1] and Paris[2] manuscripts, which were circulating in Poland in the late fifteenth century.[3] Later, in the sixteenth century, R. Vidal HaṢorfati relates in his book *Imrei Yosher* that he saw an Arabic manuscript of the work and summarises sections of it in Hebrew.

The Oxford fragment was first published in Vienna 1836 in the journal *Kerem Ḥemed*, and then reprinted in Leipzig in 1859 in a collection of the responsa of HaRaMBa"M titled *Qoveṣ Teshuvot HaRaMBa"M ve'Igerotav*.[4] In 1877 it was printed in the Vilna edition of *Ẹn Ya'ạqov* with slight emendations and copyist errors. In 1953, R. Reuven Margaliot copied the original Oxford manuscript, added citations and elucidations, and published it in his edition of Rabbenu Avraham's work *Milḥamot HaShem*.[5]

An advancement in our understanding of the original text came about when a segment of the original Judeo-Arabic work was found in the Cairo Geniza. The discovered manuscripts, subsequently divided between the Library of Westminster College in Cambridge and the library of the Alliance Israelite Universelle in Paris, contained only the middle third of the work.[6] In 1973 Rabbi Professor Elazar Hurvitz translated the Westminster College segments and published them with a comprehensive introduction

that he had included it in his own work, *Avodat HaLevi*, which has been lost.

1 A. Neubauer, *Catalogue of the Hebrew Manuscripts in the Bodleian Library*, I, 1886, col. 576, no 1649

2 Paris, Bibliothèque Nationale, Ms Héb. Ancien fonds 245, fols. 35a-40, H. Zotenberg, *Catalogues des manuscrits hébreux et samaritains de la Bibliothèque Impériale*, Paris, 1866, p. 174, no. 983.4

3 Although each manuscript contains sentences missing sentences from the other, the Hebrew is otherwise identical.

4 pp. 40b-43b

5 R. Reuven Margaliot, *Rabbenu Avraham ben HaRaMBa"M: Milḥamot Hashem*, Mossad HaRav Kook, 1953 (p.139ff.)

6 that is, the third chapter and half of the fourth chapter

in the journal *Sefer HaYovel LeYehoshuạ Finkel*,[1] and later republished it as "Treatise on Talmudic Exegesis."[2] Subsequently, Professor Paul B. Fenton discovered the Alliance Israelite Universelle fragment in their Geniza collection.

Although the original translation is generally aligned with Rabbenu Avraham's intent, it can be seen from certain segments of the Hurvitz translation that there were some deviations from the precise language and expression used by Rabbenu Avraham. As a result, some confusion may ensue in attempts to analyse and understand the exact meaning of Rabbenu Avraham's words.

In 2013, R. Moshe Meiselman published both manuscripts of the Judeo-Arabic fragments found in the Cairo Geniza in his English work *Torah, Chazal and Science*.[3] Therein, he placed three texts side by side: 1) the Judeo-Arabic fragments, 2) a scholarly translation of the Judeo-Arabic fragments,[4] and 3) the Oxford/Paris translation.

In 2019, R. Moshe Maimon produced the most impressive and extensive version to date, adding numerous sources and displaying the work's consistency with HaRaMBa"M's writings. Using the Oxford and Paris manuscripts along with R. Meiselman's scholarly translation, R. Maimon assembled a single congruent text based on what he considered to be the most reasonable assumptions regarding Rabbenu Avraham's original literary and grammatical intentions. The English language translation found in this book is based on R. Moshe Maimon's Hebrew text, including his own chapter and paragraph divisions and references.

It is our great honour to present the first fully translated edition of such a foundational work to the English speaking community. Although

1 *Derashot ḤaZa"L leRabbenu Avraham ben HaRaMBa"M*, in *Sefer HaYovel LeYehoshuạ Finkel*, Yeshiva University, New York, 1973, p.139ff.

2 in *Studies in Geonic and Rabbinic Texts from the Cairo Geniza*, New York: Yeshiva University, 1989, part II

3 Jerusalem 2013, p. 750ff.

4 translated by R. Yaakov Wincelberg and R. Pineḥas Qoraḥ

an abridged version appears in the introduction to the English edition of *Ẹn Ya'ạqov* translated by R. Shmuel Tzvi-Hirsch Glick, our goal was to accurately translate the work, word for word, to aid one engaged in the study of the Hebrew text itself. Following R. Reuven Margaliot and R. Moshe Maimon, sources and elucidations are given in the footnotes. I owe a tremendous debt of gratitude to R. Moshe Maimon for allowing me to use the Hebrew text which he polished so meticulously.

◆ ◆ ◆

Translator's Preface

Links between the Geonim and the Sepharadim

From the sixth to the eleventh century, the *Geonim*[1] headed the great *yeshivot* of Sura and Pumbedita. As spiritual heirs to the *Amora'im* and *Savora'im*, they functioned as the national leaders of the Jewish people; their interpretations of the Talmud and Rabbinic enactments came to be considered authoritative, especially throughout the Moslem-ruled world, which at the time extended from the Middle East to North Africa and Spain.

The *Geonim* made a clear distinction between *Aggada* and *Halakha*.[2] While giving ultimate authority to the halakhic sections of the Sages' writings, *aggada* was scaled down to represent only informed speculations and theories at best. This classical Geonic approach can be seen from the following sources:

> These matters, which are derived from verses and known as *midrash* and *aggada*, are only estimations, and are not akin to halakhic decision-making. [Although] some are so (meaning: literally true)... many are not...Likewise, most of the *aggadot* that the students of students said, such as Ribbi Tanḥuma and Ribbi Oshạyah and others - are not so (meaning: literally true). Therefore, we do not rely on words of *aggada*. [For only] those which are correct - [meaning] those which are actually logical and [based on] verses [do we rely on]. There is no end to *aggadot*.[3]

> You should know that the words of *aggada*[4] are not traditions, but rather interpretations of an individual's thoughts in the form of possi-

1 The plural form of *Gaon* (גאון) which means "pride" or "splendour."

2 A precedent for this approach can be found in the Jerusalem Talmud (*Pe'ah* 2:4):

Ribbi Zera [said] **in the name of Samuel: One does not rule neither from *halakhot*** (rules of practice declared in the *Mishna*) **nor from *aggadot*** (whether incorporated in the Talmud or given in separate *midrashim*), **nor from *tosafot*** (extraneous sources, *beraitot*), **but only from study** (from the Talmud, which fixes the reason for each ruling, or from a decision made by the Talmud which follows the practice of a given individual).

3 Rav Sherira Gaon, *Megilat Setarim* (no longer extant), cited in *Oṣar HaGeonim*, *Ḥagiga* 14a, p. 60

4 Here, the word *aggada* also also includes *derasha*.

bilities or suggestions, and are not set in stone.[1] Therefore, do not rely on them.[2]

> *Aggada* is any interpretation brought in the Talmud which does not deal with a commandment. This is *aggada*, and one should only learn from it when it is within reason. You should know that all laws that the Sages [of the Talmud] established on the basis of a commandment come from Moses, our teacher, may he rest in peace, who received them from the Almighty. One may neither add nor detract from them. However, when [the Sages] explain [non-legal] verses, [their statements are merely] expressions of their own opinions and views. We only learn from the interpretations that are reasonable, and do not rely on the rest.[3]

As early as the Amoraic period, we find the Spanish Jews maintaining close correspondence with the communities of Babylon. The Talmud Bavli mentions that Yiṣḥaq *Resh Galuta* (Exilarch) would travel to Spain.[4] Even after his death in Spain, a halakhic inquiry was sent from Spain to Babylon regarding the marital status of his wife.

As the old Babylon of the *Amoraim* became absorbed into the greater Arabic world due to the Islamic conquest, transmission between Sepharad and Babylon became even more transfluent. Since language and culture play a critical role in the proper transmission of any tradition from one region to another, it comes as no surprise that the linguistically and culturally Arabic society of southern Spain (Al-Andalus) would be the natural recipient of Geonic traditions from Arabic Babylonia.[5]

1 This approach is very reasonable, as we do not find that *aggadot* are written as a tradition received by a student from his teacher (as opposed to halakhic statements in the Talmud).

2 Rav Hai Gaon, cited in *Oṣar HaGeonim*, *Ḥagiga* 14a, p. 59

3 Rav Shemuel ben Ḥofni, appended after tractate *Berakhot* in the standard Vilna edition of the Talmud, translated from Arabic into Hebrew by R. Shemuel ben Ḥananya, 12th century Egypt.

4 *Yevamot* 115b

5 It is important to note that "Spain" and "Sepharad" are not precisely the same. In medieval times, Spain was generally split into two distinct geographies, the north and the south. These areas were under the control of two distinct

An outspoken proponent of the Babylonian Talmudic tradition, Pirqoi ben Baboi, already makes note of the *yeshivot* in North Africa and Sepharad:[1]

> We have heard that God granted you merit and established houses of study in all the lands of Ifriqqiya (North Africa) and in all the places of Sepharad.

R. Yehuda ben Barzilai of Barcelona (eleventh century) relates that when Shemuel HaNagid was asked directly by Rav Hai Gaon about a certain negative rumor regarding the halakhic practice of the community of Spain, Shemuel HaNagid assured Rav Hai Gaon that the Jews of Spain were meticulous in their observance of Talmudic Law, and that the Spanish community kept to a transmission of the Talmud directly from Yiṣḥaq *Resh Galuta*.[2] R. Yehudah ben Barzilai relates that Rav

---

powers (Christianity and Islam, respectively), and therefore were politically, socially, linguistically and culturally different. While Jews in southern Spain (Al-Andalus) considered themselves "Sepharadi" and were generally influenced by the Babylonian *Geonim*, the Jews in northern Spain (e.g. Catalonia) did not, and they were ideologically and methodologically closer to the neighbouring Ashkenazim of the Franco-German Rhineland. For example, the most famous northern Spaniards (RaMBa"N and RaSHB"A) introduced many Qabbalistic and Halakhic concepts of Ashkenaz into Spain. RaSHB"A was a student of R. Yonah Gerondi (foremost student of the Ashkenazi Shelomo ben Montpellier, leader of the movement against the southern Sepharadi, HaRaMBa"M) and RaMBa"N (student of Yehuda ben Yaqar, Ạzriel ben Menaḥem (student of Yiṣḥaq the Blind, amongst whom historical Qabbalah appeared), and Natan ben Meir – all students of Ashkenazi academies). This distinction between southern Spain (Al-Andalus) and northern Spain (Catalonia) is also evidenced by the fact that 'Catalonia' was not included in the denomination 'Sepharad' in medieval Hebrew works, and Catalonian Jews did not consider themselves inhabitants of Sepharad (southern Spain). We also see the distinction in the writings of the great northern Spanish scholars such as RaMBa"N and RaSHB"A, who refer to "accurate" books coming to them in northern Spain (Catalonia) from the lands of southern Spain (Al-Andalus). We also see the distinction in legal codes such as R. Yosef Qaro's Shulḥan Ạrukh, which differentiates between *minhag Sepharad* and *minhag Catalan*.

1 S. Spiegel, *"LeFarashat haPolmos shel Pirqoi ben Baboi," Harry Austryn Wolfson Jubilee Volume*, Hebrew Section (Jerusalem 1965), p. 272–273.

2 *Sefer HaỊtim*, p. 267

Naṭronai Gaon wrote the entire Talmud for the Spanish community upon visiting them.

Steady and intimate correspondence can be observed throughout the many responsa of the *Geonim.* In the mid-ninth century, Rav Ạmram Bar Sheshna Gaon composed the entire *Yesod HaẠmrami* (the oldest organized prayer book extant) specifically for the Jews of Lucena.[1] Similarly, one can see that the majority of Naṭronai ben Hilai's responsa of were addressed to the community of Lucena, a city in southern Spain.

The spreading of Geonic knowledge and methodology in Spain was enhanced by the very presence of a Babylonian Gaon who landed on the shores of southern Spain. According to legend, R. Moshe ben Ḥanokh, from one of the most important Talmudic academies in Babylonia (Sura), found himself in Andalusia after being held captive at sea in 995:

> After many days at sea, the ship cast anchor at Cordoba, Spain. Here R. Moshe and his son were quickly redeemed and set free by the Jews of Cordoba. R. Moshe and his son were so modest that they did not disclose the fact that they were great scholars.[2]

Once R. Moshe ben Ḥanokh arrived in Cordoba, he impressed the community leaders and was charged with the position of *Dayan* (judge) of the city and the *Rosh* (head) of the *yeshiva.* The work of this recently arrived Babylonian Ḥakham in Spain was greatly enhanced by a local Sepharadi Ḥakham named R. Ḥasdai ibn Shaprut, who was involved in financially supporting his efforts by purchasing copies of the Talmud from Babylonia.

1 Southeast Spain, almost exclusively inhabited by Jews. Naṭronai ben Hilai Gaon writes that "Lucena was a Jewish place, with no gentiles at all."

2 Abraham ibn Daud, *Sefer HaQabbala.* This fundamental book in the canon of the Geonic-Sepharadi tradition opens with a survey of the very earliest generations and indicates the chain by which the Law was handed down from Moses, through the men of the Great Synagogue, the Babylonian exile, the Second Temple period, the time of the Hasmoneans, then the *Tannaim, Amoraim,* and *Geonim,* the creation of new centres of learning in Egypt, Kairouan, and the western Diaspora, particularly Spain (Sepharad), to which a full third of the work is dedicated.

We begin to see many *she'elot* (questions) addressed to R. Moshe ben Ḥanokh in Spain instead of the scholars in Babylonia. The Babylonian *yeshivot* of Sura and Pumbedita were beginning to be supplanted by the Sepharadi *yeshivot* of Lucena and Cordoba.

When R. Moshe ben Ḥanokh died, much of his important work was continued by his son Ḥanokh. He produced an Arabic commentary on the Talmud[1] and wrote many responsa. The study of Talmud in Sepharad was now at an even more advanced stage.

Towards the end of the eleventh century, the *yeshivot* of Babylonia, once the main repositories of Talmudic understanding, were declining in influence, and the study of Talmud was becoming increasingly difficult. The Sepharadi *yeshivot*, which were to continue that original Geonic tradition, understood this imminent reality. Therefore, Shemuel HaNagid, a student of Ḥanokh, enhanced communication with the *Geonim* of Babylonia and their counterpart scholars of North Africa.[2] He wanted to ensure that their methodology of Talmud study and interpretation was maintained. The Geonic methodology was clear, coherent, and – importantly – was focused on *peshaṭ*.[3]

It is for this reason that Shemuel HaNagid produced an important methodological work that serves as an introduction to the Talmud, titled *Mevo HaTalmud*. He also wrote numerous responsa and halakhic compendiums, many of which have, unfortunately, been lost. His immense efforts extended to buying copies of the Talmud from Babylonia for the *yeshiva* of Cordoba, just as Ḥasdai ibn Shaprut had done. The timing was critical – by the time Shemuel HaNagid died

1 He wrote this with his contemporary, Rabbi Yosef ibn Abitur, who also lived in Cordoba (Andalusia) and was a *talmid* (student) of his father R. Moshe ben Ḥanokh.

2 The North African town of Kariouan in modern-day Tunisia was another major Torah centre that maintained correspondence with, and the tradition of, the Babylonian Geonic academies.

3 Their approach and methodology can be easily attested to from the wide range of responsa extant in our time. This approach is contrary to the *pilpul* methodology developed later in Ashkenazi academies.

(1055), the *yeshivot* of Babylonia had already been closed for almost twenty years.[1]

With the closing of these Babylonian *yeshivot*, the need for writings on Talmudic understanding and *Halakha* became even greater. Once Shemuel HaNagid died, it was left to his students to produce such works, and they rose to the task.[2] This was coupled with translations of important Geonic works from Arabic into Hebrew,[3] and commentaries on portions of the Talmud. This was followed by the production of a great commentary on the Talmud written in the eleventh century by Rabbenu Ḥananel.[4]

The importance of Rabbenu Ḥananel cannot be overstated. Not only did he produce a unique commentary on the Talmud, but he also produced a student who would become one of the most important pillars of the early Sepharadi world – R. Yiṣḥaq Alfasi (HaRI"F).

R. Yiṣḥaq Alfasi (1013-1103) was *Rosh Yeshiva* in Lucena (Andalusia), having arrived from North Africa and having been a contemporary of the last *Geonim* of Babylonia. HaRI"F soon became the rabbinic authority of his time, and the questions he received from around the world testify to his prominence beyond the borders of Spain. Notably, HaRI"F went on to produce a work of incredible magnitude, *Halakhot HaRI"F*, which is essentially an abbreviated Talmud that acted as both a code of law and a commentary. Even the halakhic authorities of France and Provence were so astonished by the magnitude of HaRI"F's achievement that Isaac the Elder (HaR"I HaZaqen), one of the great

1 Sura in 1034, and Pumbedita in 1038.

2 This includes works written by R. Yiṣḥaq ben Giat of Lucena (1030-1089) and Yiṣḥaq ibn Albalia of Cordoba (1035-1094), who wrote compilations of Halakhic collections and explanations of difficult *Halakhot*.

3 R. Yiṣḥaq Albargeloni (of Barcelona) translated an important work by Hai Gaon. The existence of such activity in Barcelona (northern Spain / Catalonia) is evidence that the study of Talmud was developing not only in the Islamic South, but also in the Christian North.

4 Written in Kairouan, north Africa. The academy of Kairouan, like those of Sepharad, maintained close contact with the Babylonian academies.

Ba'ąlei Tosafot, wrote that "it is inconceivable for a human being to compose a work like this without the *shekhinah* resting upon him."[1]

The work and traditions of HaRI"F were carried on by his student, R. Yosef ibn Migas (1077-1141). Having spent much time studying from his master, R. Yosef ibn Migas was able to interpret the Talmud and answer questions on it, as evidenced from his various responsa. Nevertheless, his veneration and allegiance to the *Geonim* was always at the forefront of his accomplishments, as he writes in a responsa:[2]

> Those who presume to rule based on thorough study of *halakha* and on the strength of their Talmudic analysis, are the ones who should be prevented from [issuing rulings], because there is no one in our current generation worthy of this and no one who has achieved, through the wisdom of the Talmud, the status of those who may issue rulings based on their own analysis, without acquainting themselves with the knowledge of the *Geonim*.

Upon the closing of the *yeshivot* in southern Spain in the twelfth century,[3] a new *yeshiva* opened in a neighboring city of exiles, thanks to Meir, son of R. Yosef ibn Migas. It is around this time that the young thirteen-year-old RaMBa"M flees his beloved Spain to Egypt, functioning as an ambassador of *Torat Sepharad* forevermore.

Descended from an illustrious rabbinic family,[4] HaRaMBa"M's father, R. Maimon, was a *Dayan* in Cordoba and a student of R. Yosef ibn Migas. Indeed, HaRaMBa"M himself regarded R. Yosef ibn Migas as his own teacher.[5] Although the *yeshivot* of Babylonia and south-

1 See Menaḥem ben Zeraḥ in his introduction to *Ṣedah LaDerekh*.

2 *Teshuvot HaR"I Migash* 114

3 Due to the activities of the fundamentalist Islamic sect, the Almohads, who persecuted the Jews of southern Spain.

4 See the conclusion of his *Commentary on the Mishnah* (tractate *Ųq'ṣin* 3:12), where HaRaMBa"M lists eight generations of his ancestry, stating that they all were distinguished *Dayanim* and Torah scholars.

5 Although in his writings HaRaMBa"M indicates that he was himself a direct student of R. Yosef ibn Migas, this is highly unlikely, for he was only six years old when R. Yosef ibn Migas passed away. His intention must be that he absorbed much of his of

ern Spain were now closed, the presence of HaRaMBa"M allowed the Geonic approach to not only survive, but to thrive through his remarkable scholarship. As he states in the introduction to his *Commentary on the Mishnah*, "I have based this work upon the words of the *Geonim*."[1]

Accordingly, the approach of the *Geonim* was manifest in the work of the great *Rishonim* of the Sepharadi region, known as Al-Andalus.[2] Aside from being the direct descendants of the Geonic approach to *Halakha*, the classical Andalusian approach, which differentiated between the fields of *Halakha* and *Midrash / Aggada* were also inherited. This can be seen from the following sources:

> These are all *midrashim*, and we are not particular to equate them with any conclusions that might logically be derived from them.[3]

> All of them are words of *aggada*, and we may not ask questions on *aggada*. For are they oral traditions or logical matters? Rather each and every person analysed the verse as they saw fit. They do not contain direct traditions, nor that which is forbidden nor permissible, nor any law. Accordingly, we do not ask questions on them...[This applies] whether they are written in the Talmud, or in books of *derashot* or *aggadot*.[4]

R. Yosef ibn Migas' tradition via the teachings of his father.

1 See also HaRaMBa"M's introduction to *Mishneh Torah*:

> ...this text will be a compilation of the entire Oral Law, along with the ordinances, customs, and decrees that were enacted from the time of Moses, our teacher, until the writing of the Talmud, as were explained by the *Geonim* in all their works, which they composed after the Talmud.

2 Jews living in the Muslim-ruled region of southern Spain (Al-Andalus) were in many ways culturally and ideologically distinct from the Jews living in the the Christian-ruled region of northern Spain (e.g. Catalonia). Further, the Jews of Christian-ruled northern Spain were generally more similar to the neighbouring Ashkenazim of the Christian-ruled Franco-German Rhineland than the Jews of Muslim-ruled region of southern Spain. The legal methodology and cultural disposition of Jews in southern Spain were deemed to be the continuation of the approach of the Babylonian *Geonim*. After their expulsion from Babylonia, many Jews settled in this southern region of Spain and established great Torah centres. See Abraham ibn Daud's *Sefer HaQabbala*.

3 Rabbenu Ḥananel, *Ḥagiga* 12a

4 HaRaMBa"M, in a letter to Pineḥas the Judge (ed. R. Shilat, p. 461). This motif is found throughout his writings.

> Many examples of this class of contradictions are found in the *Midrash* and the *Aggada*; hence the saying, "We must not raise questions concerning the contradictions met within the *Aggada*."[1]

> The exegesis [found in Rabbinic literature] that there exists a large animal [that consumes the] grazing of one thousand mountains daily[2] is delightful for the ears hearing it. Similarly a bird that covers the sun's light with its wings[3] has a secret meaning to it and is not to be taken literally.[4]

> The exegesis concerning the dots above *vaYishaqehu*[5] (*and he kissed him*) suffices for those who are drawn from the breasts.[6, 7]

> There is a third category called *Midrash*, meaning sermons. These are similar to a priest who stands up and delivers a sermon while one of the listeners, who thought it was good, wrote it down. Regarding this category, one who believes in it - good, and one who does not, will have no harm from it.[8]

Although this school of thought did not believe midrashic interpretations or aggadic narratives to be binding in any way, it nevertheless treated many of them with great veneration, believing that deeper meanings were embedded within them. Accordingly, this school maintained that those who interpreted *aggadot* literally caused mockery and desecration to the words of the Sages. HaRaMBa"M writes:[9]

1 HaRaMBa"M, *Guide*, Introduction

2 *Pirqei DeRibbi Elięzer*, chapter 11

3 *Vayiqra Rabbah*, chapter 22

4 Ibn Ęzra, Genesis 6:20

5 namely, that Esau did not kiss Jacob wholeheartedly (see Genesis 33:4)

6 meaning: children

7 Ibn Ęzra, Genesis 33:4

8 RaMBa"N, *Ma'amar HaVikuaḥ*, ed. R. Reuven Margaliot, p. 82. Although the RaMBa"N was from Catalonia, it is worth mentioning that this approach was displayed throughout the Iberian peninsula, even by those who were more mystically inclined.

9 *Commentary to the Mishna, Pereq Ḥeleq*

And [the members of the group who grasp the truth and understand the greatness of the Sages] know that [the Sages], peace be upon them, do not speak words of mockery; for they know that their (the Sages') words contain [both] a revealed and a hidden [meaning], and when they (the Sages) spoke of impossible matters, they were speaking by way of a riddle and a parable - for this is the way of the wisest men. For this reason, the greatest of wise men began his book by saying *To understand a parable and a metaphor - the words of wise and their riddles.*[1] And it is known to linguists that a riddle pertains to its hidden [meaning] and not to that which is revealed. As it says, *Let me present a riddle before you*...For the objective of the Sages' words was to elucidate metaphysical matters, [hidden as] riddles and parables. And why should we be astonished towards them (the Sages) for writing esoteric matters in the way of parables, making it appear as lower things to the masses? for behold, we see that the wisest of all men did this with Divine help - meaning Solomon, in Proverbs, and in Song of Songs, and in some of Ecclesiastes. And why should it be strange for us to explain their words rationally and to take them out of their simple meaning in order that they become reasonable and correspond to the truth and to Holy Scriptures? For they (the Sages) themselves explain verses of Scripture rationally and take them out of their simple meaning and make them into parables...

DIFFERENCES BETWEEN THE ASHKENAZI AND THE GEONIC-SEPHARADI APPROACH

While the *Rishonim* of Al-Andalus lived during the cultural peak of the Islamic world's contribution to astronomy, mathematics, science, medicine, and philosophy, the *Rishonim* of Germany and France, living within Christendom, had limited access to these sciences and were generally unfamiliar with these lines of thought.[2]

1 Proverbs 1:6

2 See R. Yehuda Ibn Tibon in his introduction to *Ḥovot HaLevavot*:

And in the lands of Edom [Christian lands wherein the Ashkenazim resided] there was refuge to the rest of our nation. They had great Sages in the wisdom of Torah and Talmud since the days of yore; however, they did not engage in other wisdoms because their Torah was their livelihood and because books of other wisdoms were unavailable to them.

Their respective approaches to world wisdoms also reflected their diametrically different world views. Whereas the Andalusian sages viewed the various wisdoms as

A possible corollary to this was the general acceptance of *midrashim* and *aggadot* at face value, without regard for the problem of puzzling or impossible matters. Whereas the Andalusian school of thought may interpret a certain *midrash* or *aggada* as a riddle and parable, the *Rishonim* of Ashkenaz would interpret it literally, and relate to it as they did to halakhic literature. As a result, halakhic matters would often be derived from sources that the Andalusian sages would not use, as can be seen in the examples below:

Birkat Kohanim

Regarding a *kohen* who does not perform the Priestly Benediction, the Talmud states:[1]

> **Any priest who does not go up to the platform** [to bless the people] **violates three positive** [*miṣvot*]: **"So you shall bless,"**[2] **"And you shall say to them,"**[3] [and] **"So shall they put My name."**[4]

Since the Talmud does not limit this to any specific *kohen*, it would seemingly apply to any *kohen* of the age of *Bar Miṣva*. However, based on a *midrash* that states "any man who does not have a wife is left without joy,"[5] Mordekhai ben Hillel HaKohen (known as MoRDKH"I) and Ṣediqiah ben Avraham Ạnav (known for his work *Shibolei HaLeqeṭ*) codify[6] that an unmarried *kohen* does not perform the priestly benediction, since we find that Isaac blessed Jacob only after he ate,[7] and since the Children of Israel blessed King Solomon when they were "joyful

different expressions of the Divine, forming an integral part of their service to God, the scholars of the Christian lands generally approached anything seemingly outside the realm of Torah as a possible distraction and even as a threat to the true service of God.

1 *Soṭa* 38b

2 Numbers 6:23

3 ibid.

4 Numbers 6:27

5 *Yevamot* 62b

6 see *Bet Yosef*, *Oraḥ Ḥayim* 128:63

7 Genesis 27:7

and glad of heart."[1] However, regarding this ruling, R. Shelomo ben Avraham ibn Aderet writes:

> I have never heard this ruling mentioned from our teachers. Perhaps it is a *midrash aggada*. But, according to our Talmud, it does not seem so, as it was not mentioned anywhere.[2]

Similarly, the Talmud states that *kohanim* are to lift their hands and align them with their shoulders during *Birkat Kohanim*,[3] but the position of the fingers is never specified. However, according to the Ashkenazi rite, the *kohanim* spread their fingers,[4] based on the following *midrash*:[5]

> God told them (the Jewish people): Although I told the *kohanim* to bless you, together with them I stand and bless you. Therefore, the priests spread their hands to show that God stands behind them, and for this reason the verse states[6] *Gazing through the window* - between the shoulders of the priests, *Peering through the lattice*[7] - between the fingers of priests.

However, see *Bet Yosef*,[8] who after citing the above opinion writes, "But HaRaMBa"M did not mention this at all since it is not mentioned in the Talmud." Conceivably, HaRaMBa"M did not see that *derasha* as a halakhic source, and thus did not mention or recognize these customs in *Mishneh Torah*.[9]

1 I Kings 8:66

2 see *Bet Yosef*, ibid.

3 *Soṭa* 38a

4 *Pisqei HaRO"SH, Megila* 3:21, MoRDeKH"I 3:816, Rabbenu Tam (*Ṣeror HaḤayim*, Jerusalem 5726, p. 17)

5 *Bamidbar Rabbah* 11:2

6 Song of Songs 2:9

7 ibid.

8 *Oraḥ Ḥayim* 128:22

9 Although the *Bet Yosef* implies that if the *midrash* was in the Talmud it would be binding, from the above sources we can deduce that even if it appeared in the Talmud,

Seụda Shelishit

It is stated in *Midrash Tehilim*,[1] "Any person who drinks water during twilight steals from his dead." Based on this, Rabbenu Tam derives that it is forbidden to eat *Seụda Shelishit* between *Minḥa* and *Ạrvit*. Contrary to this, HaRaMBa"M[2] writes specifically that the custom of the righteous is to eat *Seụda Shelishit* between *Minḥa* and *Ạrvit*.

Immersion in a River

The Talmud[3] states that Rav believes that rainwater increases the water flow in the Euphrates River, and thus forbids immersion in it, since the river may be composed of a majority of rainwater, rendering an immersion invalid, whereas Shemuel believes that the increase in the Euphrates' water flow is attributable to its tributaries, and thus permits immersion in it. Although the Talmud states that Shemuel's own father followed Rav's opinion, and that Shemuel himself was stringent in a different situation, Rabbenu Tam codified the *halakha* in accordance with Shemuel's lenient opinion, on the basis of two *midrashim* that correspond to it.[4] However, Rabbenu Ḥananel, the RI"F, and HaRaMBa"M[5] all decide according to Rav, especially in light of the rule that the *halakha* always follows Rav over Shemuel in ritual law (*Issur veHeter*). Regarding this, the RaMBa"N stated, "We do not push aside a teaching of ritual matter and law because of one Aggadic teaching."[6]

HaRaMBa"M would still not learn from it, for it is within the category of *aggada* or *derasha*. See below, p. *lii* (Customs based on Aggada), where it is explained that even HaRamBa"M would associate certain customs with *midrashim*. Nevertheless, this was done with much reservation and only already-widespread customs were treated in this manner. Additionally, *midrashim* would not be used as halakhic sources vis à vis the Talmud.

1 *Midrash Shoḥar Ṭov* 11:6

2 *Hilkhot Shabbat* 30:10

3 *Nedarim* 40b

4 see Ra"N, ibid.

5 *Hilkhot Miqvaot* 9:13

6 RaMBa"N on the RI"F - *Nedarim* 13a

Intimate Relations During a Famine

The Talmud states:[1]

> **It is prohibited for a person to have conjugal relations in years of famine, as it is stated,** *And to Yosef were born two sons before the year of famine came.*[2] **It was taught:** [Nevertheless,] **those without children may have marital relations in years of famine.**

And so codifies HaRaMBa"M:[3]

> And it is forbidden for anyone who has fulfilled the commandment of being fruitful and multiplying to engage in marital relations in years of famine.

However, Tosafot questions this ruling based upon an exegesis stating that Yokheved was conceived as Jacob and his family descended to Egypt, and was born upon their arrival in Egypt.[4] For, since it was a year of famine, asks the Tosafot, how did Levi (the father of Yokheved) have conjugal relations? To solve this contradiction, the Tosafot answer the aforementioned principle by changing the Talmudic dictum from a law to merely an extra level of piety which Yosef chose to practice. Notably, both Ibn Ẹzra and Rabbenu Avraham ben HaRaMBa"M disagree with the exegesis given for the dates regarding Yokheved.[5]

A Husband who is Abroad

The Talmud states that if a woman was found to be pregnant while her husband was abroad, the child is a *mamzer*.[6] However, based upon a ruling of Rava Tosfa'a who rendered fit a child who was delayed in its mothers womb for twelve months since the husband is presumed to be

1 *Taạnit* 11a

2 Genesis 41:50

3 *Hilkhot Taạnit* 3:8

4 *Bava Batra* 120a

5 Genesis 46:27

6 *Qidushin* 73a

the father,[1] HaRaMBa"M codifies: "A fetus will not remain in its mother's womb for more than twelve months."[2]

However, based upon a certain Aggadic narrative which states that the father of Shemuel (Aba bar Aba) was able to visit his wife from abroad through the use of a Divine Name, Tosafot concludes that that a child can be considered fit even if it was born after the twelfth month, provided that the mother claims that her husband visited her by use of a Divine Name.[3]

Ṣiṣit for an Unmarried Man

An even more novel position of this approach is the use of post-Talmudic *derashot* for halakhic considerations. For example, many Ashkenazi *Rishonim*[4] state that the custom is to refrain from wearing a *ṭalit*[5] before marriage, since the Torah juxtaposes the laws of *ṣiṣit* - *you shall make for yourself fringes*[6] - with marriage - *if a man shall take a woman,*[7] implying that a man need not wear a *ṭalit* until he gets married. This *derasha* is nowhere to be found in any book of *Midrash*,[8] and is at odds with the Talmud, which states[9] that even a child under than the age of *Bar Miṣva* is obligated in wearing a *ṭalit*: "A minor who knows how to wrap himself in a garment is obligated in the *miṣva* of *ṣiṣit*."[10]

---

1 *Yevamot* 80b

2 *Hilkhot Isurei Bia* 15:19

3 *Qidushin* 73a

4 See *Tashbeṣ Qaṭan* 464 and MaHaRI"L, *Hilkhot Ishut* 10.

5 From the above sources, the custom excluded any type of *ṭalit*, whether it be a *ṭalit gadol* or *ṭalit qaṭan*.

6 Deuteronomy 22:13

7 Deuteronomy 22:12

8 It should be noted that R. Avraham ben Natan (*Sefer HaManhig: Hilkhot Erusin veNisuin* 108) cites an ambiguous *midrash* which makes this juxtaposition; however, it only derives from there that a groom should wear a *ṭalit* under the *ḥupa*.

9 *Sukkah* 42a

10 Although those who follow this custom in our time do allow unmarried boys to wear

Attending Medical School

The literal approach to *Midrash* and *Aggada* is seen in modern halakhic literature. For example, when R. Moshe Feinstein was asked about Yeshiva students who desired to leave Yeshiva in order to study medicine at university, he replied:

> And know, my honorable friend, that those in our generations and even in previous generations, for approximately the past two hundred years, who chose the occupation of being a doctor, did not do so because they are naturally suited towards it, but because it is a respected (occupation) by the general Jewish and gentile population, and since it is an honoured profession with generous remuneration. Thus, that which the *Ḥovot HaLevavot* mentions in the third chapter of *Sha'ar HaBiṭaḥon* - "Every man has a preference for a particular work or business over others. G-d has already implanted in his nature a love and fondness for it etc...One who finds his nature and personality attracted to a certain occupation, and his body is suited for it, that he will be able to bear its demands - he should pursue it, and make it his means of earning a livelihood" - only applies to that which can possess a natural attraction due to a person's inherent makeup, and not because he knows that this type of occupation is respectable and will bring great fortune, for that type of attraction and desire is nothing. In fact, it seems to me that an occupation in medicine is not an inherent natural tendency embedded in mankind. For when the author wrote *Ḥovot HaLevavot*, the wisdom of medicine was a common occupation of Torah scholars, especially for the sages of Spain, where the author, Rabbenu Baḥya, lived. And [nevertheless] he did not mention the occupation of medicine amongst the occupations mentioned at the beginning of this segment. It therefore seems that medicine as an occupation is not included in this matter, for a person does not have a natural tendency towards it. And the reason for this seems simple, for medicine was not a natural [necessity] in the beginning of creation, for it was not inherent for a person to become ill. For

a *ṭalit qaṭan*, many authorities believe that only a garment which can be wrapped around the entire body suffices for the *miṣva* (*Teshuvot HaRaMBa"M*, Blau, 220; *HaMaspiq LeOvde Hashem*, Dana, p. 269). Ostensibly, the above passage from the Talmud would not be referring to the *ṭalit qaṭan*, which is a post-Talmudic invention.

> though death was decreed on the first day of Creation immediately after Adam ate from the Tree of Knowledge, sickness did not occur until Jacob came and prayed for mercy and sickness came about. And until Elishạ, one did not fall ill and then heal [as everyone who fell ill died]. [Then] Elishạ came and prayed for mercy and was healed, as is brought in *Bava Meṣia* 87a and *Sanhedrin* 107b. Therefore a love and fondness for medicine can not be implanted in a person's nature. For all the love and fondness towards medicine only comes from the respectable and great income it brings. And if there was another respectable occupation that brings a better income, there would not be any desire to become a doctor and deal with the sick.[1]

As can be seen, R. Moshe Feinstein understood the *midrash* brought in *Bava Meṣia* as a historical reality and even used it as a guiding factor in choosing one's professional field.[2]

1 *Igrot Moshe* VIII, *Yoreh Deạh* 4:36

2 The difficulty with R. Feinstein's approach is that there exist conflicting *midrashim*. For example, in *Bava Batra* (16b) Rabbi Shimon ben Yoḥai states, "A precious stone hung around the neck of Avraham our forefather and any sick person who looked at it would immediately be healed." This contradicts the *midrash* brought in *Bava Meṣia* which states that there was no sickness until Jacob prayed. Tosafot (*Bava Batra* ibid.) takes note of this and offers two possible solutions:

> We can say that here (regarding Avraham), we are dealing with an illness due to a physical injury. [Alternatively] Rabbenu Tam and Rabbenu Yiṣḥaq explain that until Jacob no one became weak, meaning mortally ill. From then onwards, there was mortal illness, and no one was able to recover until Elishạ.

According to both of these answers, doctors would still have been necessary since the beginning of time, in contradiction to the approach of R. Feinstein. Nevertheless, even the two solutions of the Tosafot do not suffice to answer a different *midrash* brought in *Bereshit Rabbah* 53:13 [see also RaSH"I on Genesis 21:14]: "Sarah had cast an evil eye upon him (Ishmael), so that a fever seized him and he was in pain…for it is normal for a sick person to drink plenty throughout the day."

According to this *midrash*, neither of the answers of Tosafot would suffice, since (a) it was not a physical injury, and (b) it was a mortal illness, as Hagar stated "Let me not look on as the child dies." In order to solve this problem, the Ḥizquni (ibid.) builds upon the answer of Rabbenu Tam and Rabbenu Yiṣḥaq by adding another exception: "We must assume that the Talmud refers to terminal sickness, but that did not include dying from thirst." Nevertheless, according to the approach of the *Geonim* and *Rishonim* of Al-Andalus, questions like this would never transpire, as HaRaMBa"M stated above: "We may not ask questions on *aggada*."

Panim Ḥadashot

The Talmud states[1] that *Birkat Ḥatanim* (*Shevạ Berakhot*) is recited in a quorum of ten men on each of the seven days of the wedding celebration. The Talmud qualifies this ruling with a statement of Rav Yehuda; namely, that only when new faces (*panim ḥadashot*) join the celebration is the *Birkat Ḥatanim* recited: Unlike HaRaM-Ba"M, who explains[2] that *panim ḥadashot* are individuals who did not hear the recitation of the *Shevạ Berakhot* at the wedding, the Tosafot[3] explain *panim ḥadashot* to be individuals who enhance the celebration.

According to this understanding, the Tosafot advances to say that the Sabbath is also considered *panim ḥadashot*, based on a aggadic passage which states,[4] "*A song for the day of the Sabbath*[5] – God says, 'new faces [*panim ḥadashot*] have arrived here, let us sing song.'" Since the passage refers to the Sabbath as *panim ḥadashot*, the Tosafot deduce that physical *panim ḥadashot* are not required for the recitation of *Birkat Ḥatanim* on the Sabbath. The reason, the Tosafot explain, is that a meal in honor of a bride and groom which occurs on the Sabbath has an added dimension of food and joy (due to the honor of the Sabbath); this increased level of joy acts as *panim ḥadashot*, thus fulfilling the requirements for reciting *Birkat Ḥatanim*.[6]

1 *Ketubot* 7b

2 *Hilkhot Berakhot* 2:10

3 *Ketubot* 7b

4 R. Shiloh Refael (*RaSHB"A* – Mossad HaRav Kook, footnote 400) notes that *Sefer HaManhig* sources this aggadic passage to the Jerusalem Talmud and *Bereshit Rabbah*. He also states that the Meiri sources it to *Midrash Tehilim*. R. Yiṣḥaq Refael (ibid. note 44) states that we do not currently have these sources before us.

5 Psalms 92

6 See *Shulḥan Ạrukh, Even Ha'Ẹzer* 62:8, where this is cited as a second opinion and as the common custom.

The Blessing "HaNoten LaYa'ef Koaḥ"

Rabbenu Ya'aqov ben Asher writes that a certain blessing recited by those of Ashkenaz was inspired by a *midrash*:[1]

> There is one more blessing found in the prayer book according to the Ashkenazi rite: *Barukh atah...HaNoten LaYa'ef Koaḥ*. It was established based on the idea that in the evening, one entrusts his soul into the hands of God, tired from a full day of work, yet [God] returns it to him in the morning, rejuvenated. This is based on the *Midrash*: "*Each morning refreshed, Your faithfulness is immense.*[2] [When a person of] flesh and blood places a deposit in the hands of his friend, [his friend] returns it worn out and damaged. However, when one entrusts his exhausted soul each evening into the hand of God, [God] returns it to him in the morning anew and rejuvenated."

However, many authorities write that blessings absent in the Talmud many not be recited,[3] as Rabbi Yosef Qaro comments:[4]

> Although there is a beautiful reference for the recitation of this blessing, since it is not found in the Talmud, I do not know how anyone was permitted to enact it.[5]

---

1 *Arba'ah Ṭurim, Oraḥ Ḥayim* 46

2 Lamentations 3:23

3 See *Responsa of RaSH"I* 91:

> It is completely forbidden to recite [the blessing of] *Yir'u Ẹnenu*, since it is not written in the Talmud, and is [thus] a blessing in vain.

Similarly, Rabbenu Avraham ben HaRaMBa"M writes in his responsa (83):

> And we have already seen [that] all the blessings which you wrote in your question, [are] blessings which we do not know their source or beginning, such as *Magbiah Shefalim* after *Zokef Kefufim*, which were not mentioned in the Talmud. [Even] if they are mentioned in a liturgical compendium, they are mistakes of a scribe or sage or cantor, and are forbidden to recite, and it is so for any new addition to the [existing] blessings.

However, see Meiri (*Berakhot* 4a), who explains why some *Geonim* were of the opinion that the leaders of each generation could enact new *berakhot*.

4 *Bet Yosef, Oraḥ Ḥayim* 46

5 R. Yoel Sirkis (*Bayit Ḥadash* 46:13) suggests that this blessing must have been found in the text of the Talmud of those who mentioned it, and even proposes reading R. Ya'aqov ben Asher's inclusion of it as confirmation to this theory. Nevertheless, this proposition is hard to accept, for if that was the case, R. Ya'aqov (along with

SEEMING CONTRADICTIONS

In *Darkhe Hora'a*, R. Tzvi Hirsch Chajes demonstrates how numerous laws are indeed derived from various *aggadot* mentioned in the Talmud.[1] Although most of the examples he gives are not from the Andalusian school of thought, one example comes from HaRaMBa"M:[2]

> A gentile is executed by the testimony of one witness, and with one judge, without forewarning, and by the testimony of relatives, but not by the testimony of a woman.

However, the source for this ruling comes from the Talmud in *Sanhedrin*:[3]

> Rabbi Ya'aqov bar Aḥa found it written in a book of *aggadot* in the study hall of Rav: A descendant of Noaḥ is executed on the basis of one judge, and by (the testimony of) one witness, and without being given forewarning. By the mouth of a man and not by the mouth of a woman; and even a relative (may judge or testify against him).

Since this law was only mentioned in a book of *aggadot* found in the study hall of Rav,[4] R. Tzvi Hirsch Chajes asserts that this is the most convincing proof that *halakhot* may be derived from any *aggadot* brought in the Talmud.

However, one may simply posit that—although the teaching was found in an aggadic work— since it is brought in the context of *Halakha*, it was, in actuality, ratified as *Halakha*. Alternatively, HaRaMBa"M may have relied on the Jerusalem Talmud, which also states[5] that a gentile is executed by the testimony of one witness and one judge and without warning.

any other earlier authority who quotes this blessing) would have mentioned this important factor.

1 *Darkhe Hora'a* II

2 *Hilkhot Melakhim* 9:14

3 *Sanhedrin* 57b

4 See also *Bereshit Rabbah, Noaḥ* 34:14, which states a similar teaching in the name of Ribbi Ḥanina.

5 *Qidushin* 1:11 (However, it does not mention anything about the testimony of relatives or a woman.)

CUSTOMS BASED ON AGGADA

Although the Andalusian approach does not derive *halakhot* from *aggadot*, we nevertheless do find that customs can be associated with *aggadot*.

Reciting "Barukh Shem Kevod..." during Shemạ Yisrael

The Talmud[1] asks what is the reason why *"Barukh shem kevod malkhuto le'ọlam vaẹd"* is recited in the *Shemạ*, despite its absence from the Torah. The Talmud answers:

> Ya'ạqov wanted to reveal to his sons the end of days, but the Divine Presence left him (rendering him unable to prophesy). He said: Perhaps, Heaven forfend, one of my descendants is unfit, (in a) similar (manner) to (what happened to) Avraham, from whom Ishmael emerged, and like my father Yiṣḥaq, from whom Esau emerged. His sons said to him, *Hear Israel, the Lord is our God, the Lord is One.* They said: Just as there is only One (God) in your heart, so too, there is only One in our hearts. At that moment Ya'ạqov our forefather said, *"Barukh shem kevod malkhuto le'ọlam vaẹd"* (blessed be the name of His glorious kingdom for ever and ever).

HaRaMBa"M relates this story,[2] and then writes, "therefore, all Jews are accustomed to utter the praise that Israel, the elder, uttered after this verse."

Checking Lungs following Sheḥiṭah

According to the letter of the law, after the slaughter of any animal, its lungs would not require checking for any adhesions, for the presumption that the majority of animals are healthy can be relied upon.[3] Nevertheless, the *Midrash Tanḥuma* states:[4]

> When a Jew takes an animal that is either a sheep, goat, or lamb, [he first] slaughters it, skins it, and places his hands inside and

1 *Pesaḥim* 56a

2 *Hilkhot Qeriyat Shemạ* 1:4

3 See *Kesef Mishneh, Hilkhot Sheḥiṭah* 11:7

4 *Shemini* 8

> examines the lung. If it is found to be a *ṭerefa*, he leaves it and does not eat from it.

Accordingly, HaRaMBa"M writes:[1]

> The widespread custom among the Jewish people is as follows: When a domesticated animal or a wild beast is slaughtered, we tear open the diaphragm and check the lung in its place...

CONCLUSIONS

As is seen from the above examples, the difference in approach towards *Midrash* and *Aggada* resulted not only in philosophical variances, but even in halakhic variances. Whereas the general approach of the *Rishonim* of Ashkenaz was to treat midrashic and halakhic discussion as equally authoritative and interrelated, the Geonic–Sepharadi tradition approached them as two separate genres, not to be intermingled.[2]

CLOSING THOUGHTS

Rabbenu Avraham ben HaRaMBa"M should be an inspiration for all. Whereas the Jewish community tends to split into polarised extremes, Rabbenu Avraham ben HaRaMBa"M displays a balanced approach which celebrates the highest levels of spirituality, piety, halakhic observance, and rational knowledge, without over-zealous partisanship, but also without compromise.

◆ ◆ ◆

1 See *Peri Megadim*, introduction to *Siman* 39, where he tries to explain that, in reality, HaRaMBa"M is of the opinion that one is obligated to check. Nevertheless, the simple understanding is that of the *Kesef Mishneh* (ibid.).

2 It should be noted that the diverging approaches to *midrash* / *aggada* are no longer exclusive to the decendents or regions of old Sepharad and Ashkenaz. For we find great Sepharadi *Aḥaronim*, such as Rabbi Ḥayim Yosef David Azulai (see *Ḥayim Sha'al*, I, 92), Rabbi Ḥezekiah da Silva (*Mayim Ḥayim*, *Berakhot*, chapter 5), and Rabbi Ḥayim Palachi (*Lev Ḥayim*, III, 99), who derive *halakhot* from *midrashim* when they do not contradict rulings from the Talmud. In contrast, great Ashkenazi *Aḥaronim*, such as Rabbi Yeḥezqel Landau (*Nodạ BeYehudah*, *Yoreh De'ạh* 161) and Rabbi Yom Ṭov Lipmann Heller, (*Tosafot Yom Tov*, *Berakhot* 5:4) write that *halakhot* cannot be learned from *midrashim*, for they were written only for ethical and allegorical purposes. However, it is worth noting where each respective approach originated, in the formative years of Sepharad and Ashkenaz.

Editor's Preface

The sphere of conviction

למען הודיעך כי לא על הלחם לבדו יחיה האדם כי על כל מוצא פי יהוה יחיה האדם

דברים ח:ג

that he might make thee know that man doth not live by bread only, but by every word that proceedeth out of the mouth of the LORD doth man live.

Deuteronomy 8:3

In the early stages of the Enlightenment, humanity began waking up to the nature of the universe. Even the most credible cosmological conceptions of the time were not left unscathed. Man began to realise his minuteness, and with time he would see himself shrink yet further.

The effect of these discoveries extended far beyond changes in scientists' methods for calculating obscure planetary movements: The bedrock upon which society rested had been suddenly and catastrophically upended. Man went from being the obvious center of the cosmos to being a mere speck in the vast universe. The orderly, just cosmos became an infinite morass of unbending laws which did not display compassion for its inhabitants.

Confronting this new problem of apparent insignificance would have been trying enough as it was, even if humanity had fully united to do so. Alas, unity, as it does in our time, remained elusive. The Church persecuted tens, if not hundreds, of so-called scientist "heretics," who, by mere observation of astronomical phenomena, had gravely sinned against official doctrines.[1]

The Church, and much of society at large, saw these and myriad others of new scientific advancements as irreconcilably opposed to

1 The most well-known case of Church persecution of a scientist is the Galileo affair. For a brief yet thorough history of this affair, see Maurice A. Finocchiaro's introduction to his book *The Galileo Affair: A Documentary History*, sections 4-8.

faith. What had thus far been the domain of the Divine – namely, unknowable mystery guided by God, perfectly executed in the service of each individual's destiny – was now posited as existing within the opposing domain of science.

It was a zero-sum game: whenever the sphere of science gained, the sphere of the Divine lost. Eventually, religious society would come to terms with the realities staring it in the face, proven beyond a doubt. The Church was severely weakened by its clash with the world of the scientific age. The rational mind rejected fantasies and derided them as primitive and simplistic. Ideas which openly contradicted known and proven facts had no place in this new epoch, in which humanity had began harnessing nature to plow the fields of progress.

Many religious institutions fall prey to a faith based on all that which is mysterious and unknown. Given a society in which the mysterious is being demystified and the unknown is becoming known, this is an unsustainable approach. For adopting this approach, especially in a post-Enlightenment world, ensures that the sphere of conviction shrinks and collapses. The more that is known, the less that is ascribed to God.

The classical Sepharadi approach to *Midrash* and *Aggadah*, a heritage of the *Geonim* so clearly articulated by Rabbenu Avraham ben HaRaMBa"M in the chapter presented here, encourages engagement with reality. Yet more importantly, this approach is nested within the greater classical Sepharadi message: know the Creator through His creations. The natural world, in all its beauty, is where humans must go not to ridicule the Divine, not to behold its contradiction, but to recognize and appreciate it. The more humanity understands about the world it inhabits, the more harmony is realized, and the more potential there is to appreciate God's creations. Thus does the sphere of conviction increase. Torah and the natural world complement each other in a positive-sum game.

What, then, can we say of *Midrash* and *Aggadah*? How are these canonical categories, at times seemingly whimsical and fantastical, to be viewed considering the instruction to embrace reality?

Man doth not live by bread alone. It is arguable that the most fundamental distinction between man and beast is the power of conscious, articulated thought. Instinct shares space with the faculty of abstraction, which allows man to learn from his surroundings in a manner in which beast cannot. The Geonic-Sepharadi tradition sees *Midrash* and *Aggadah* as wellsprings of abstraction and symbol which, instead of providing fertile ground for claims of primitivity, are seen as expressing deep truths about the human psyche, which lives in symbol and story.

The critical mind of our time will rejoice in the discovery and implementation of this approach, for it vests the vast oceans of our tradition with renewed wisdom. It is my hope that the publication of this chapter will enlighten a new generation of readers unto the wisdom contained in the Midrashic and Aggadic heritage of our nation.

May our spheres of conviction expand, and may we all go from strength to strength.

Avner Yeshurun
Editor

Avraham ben HaRaMBa"M

Understanding *Ḥaza"l*

◆◆◆

החסיד רבנו אברהם בן הרמב"ם

מאמר על הדרשות ועל האגדות

◆◆◆

מקרא: גוף הטקסט מודפס בגופן כזה [והוספות ע"פ כת"י כמו שנדפסו ע"י פרופ' הורביץ והר"מ מייזלמאן סומנו במרובעיים כאלו]. **ציטוטים, וכן ניבים וביטויים שיש לשער שנכתבו בראשונה בלה"ק, באותיות מודגשות כאלו.** {הוספות לנוחיות הקריאה הוכנסו בתוך סוגריים עקומות כאלו}. (כנהוג, מחיקות וט"ס הן בתוך סוגריים עגולות כאלו), [ותיקונים ע"פ השערה בגוף הטקסט באות אחריהן בגופן כזה בתוך מרובעיים כאלו]. מראה מקומות נדפסו כהערות בסוף הספר, ובגוף הטסקט סומנו באות בכתב רש"י.

Chapter 1: Introduction

The need for proper guidance in the study of midrashic and aggadic passages

Let it be known that everything in the Talmud or in the other writings of the Sages [concerning] *midrashim*[1] and *aggadot*[2] contains very few commentaries currently in our possession.[3] [These few commentaries] are unknown to those who study the Talmud, and [even] the majority of [these] commentators did not attempt to make sense of their meaning.

My father, my master, of blessed memory, conceived of composing a book for their explanation - as he mentioned in the beginning of [*Pereq Ḥeleq* in his] *Commentary to the Mishna*,[4] but withdrew from it out of apprehension,[5] as he mentioned in the beginning of the *Guide for the Perplexed*.[6] After his death, I began writing nominally upon this

1 The term *Midrashim* refers to rabbinic works which interpret Scripture. Henceforward, they will be described by the term *exegeses*.

2 The term *Aggadot* refers to independent non-legalistic works which contain anecdotes, accounts, and lessons on a varying, wide range of topics. Henceforward, they will be described by the term *narratives*.

3 See *Milḥamot HaShem* (R. Margaliot, p. 49) where he refers to "commentaries" such as those of Rabbenu Nissim Gaon, author of *Megilat Setarim*, and Rabbenu Ḥananel.

4 "I shall yet write a composition in which I will gather all the exegeses found in the Talmud and in other [works], and I will elucidate them and explain them such that they shall be reconciled with the truth of [their] matters, and I will also provide proofs [to my explanations] from their words. I will reveal which of the exegeses are to be understood simply, and which are parables, and which were dreams [despite] their portrayal as simple statements, as if they occurred in reality. In that composition, I shall elucidate for you myriad opinions, and there I shall elucidate all of the principles which I have given you, [including] some from here, [so that you may] extrapolate from them to the others."

5 In the Hebrew version he states poetically "ויירא משה מגשת אליו", "and Moses feared to come near it," based on Exodus 34:30.

6 "We have already determined, in our commentary to the Mishna, that we will explain strange matters in the Book of Prophecy and in the Book of Harmony - we determined to examine, in these books, all matters of exegesis which, if taken literally, distance one considerably from truth and are removed of intelligence, and which

פרק א: פתיחה

הצורך בהדרכה נכונה ללימוד מדרשים ואגדות

דע, כי כל הנמצא בתלמוד וזולתו מחיבורי החכמים ז"ל {בענין} מדרשות והמעשיות {=מדרשים ואגדות} - דברי הפירושים {עליהם} הנמצאים בידינו עתה הם מעטים, ו{הם} נעלמים מעיני כל ההוגים בתלמוד, ורובי המפרשים לא שלחו בהם ידם, ולא באה נפשם בסודם.

ואבא מרי ז"ל חשב לחבר ספר בפירושם - כאשר זכר בתחילת {פרק חלק מ}פירוש המשנה, ואמנם לבסוף נטה מעליו, וייראו משה מגשת אליו[6] - כאשר אמר בתחלת המורה. ואני אחר פטירתו פירשתי בענין זה מעט קט, ו{אמנם} לא נשלם מפני

matter; however, I was unable to complete [the task] due to my preoccupation in composing this book,[1] for I saw the benefit of the latter would be greater than that of the former. Nevertheless, I will arouse your heart and thoughts [regarding the fundamental principles].

Take heed of this [correct] approach, [in order to properly] understand that which the Sages stated in their exegeses, and from it you shall see their [true] intention. [As a result,] *He shall be your God and you shall be his spokesman.*[2] By virtue [of what I will explain to you], you will be freed from mocking the words of the Sages or from denying the truth of their words.[3]

You will be freed from thinking that these [exegeses] are [filled with] miracles equivalent to those performed on behalf of the Prophets.[4] [As a result, you will not think] that similar [miracles] will be performed on behalf of every sage or pious individual.[5] [You will not think] that there is no difference between the splitting of the Sea of

are entirely figurative. When I began, many years ago, to compile these works, I proceeded to write a portion of them, but became dissatisfied with our exposition of these passages in this manner, for we have seen that if we were to expound them by means of allegory and conceal that which is to be concealed, we do not explain anything, but merely substitute one thing for another of the same nature. And if I were to fully explain what must be explained, it would not suit most people; and my sole object in writing those books was to make the contents of *midrashim* and the exoteric lessons of the prophecies intelligible to all."

1 His magnum opus, *Kifāyat al-ʿĀbidīn (HaMaspiq LeOvde HaShem)*, from which this chapter is extracted.

2 based on Exodus 4:16

3 Taking *midrashim* literally can generate disdain towards the Sages, as intelligent people often liken such *midrashim* to common legends, myths, and fantasies.

4 When taken literally, many *midrashim* contain miraculous stories that parallel or even supersede those which occur in Scripture. As a result, actual Biblical miracles become anticlimactic. See below, chapter 4, for the way in which Rabbenu Avraham interprets seemingly miraculous events recorded in the Talmud. This understanding is in line with HaRaMBa"M' reservation accepting the credulous opinion that a certain event was miraculous; see *Epistle of the Resurrection of the Dead* (ed. Qafiḥ, *Igerot HaRaMBa"M*, p. 88)

5 As the masses often believe that pious individuals must be capable of performing miracles, since the works of the Sages are filled with such stories.

שנתעסקתי בחבור הספר הזה, כי ראיתי תועלתו גדולה ונאמנה {יותר} **מתועלת (הראשונה) [הראשון],** {אבל} **אעפ"כ אני מעיר לבך ורעיונך** {על עיקרי הדברים}.

ואתה פקח עיניך על הדרך הזה, {שהוא הדרך הנכון להבין מה} **שדברו החכמים בדרשות הנמצאות להם, וממנו כוונתם תהא צופה, ויהיה לך לאלהים ואתה תהיה לו לפה.**[ה] **ומזה** {שאבאר} **תמלט נפשך מלהלעיג על דברי החכמים או מלכפור באמיתת דבריהם, או** {תמלט נפשך} **משתחשוב שהם מעשה נסים כאשר נעשה לנביאים, ו**{לא תחשוב} **כי כן יעשה לכל חכם וחסיד, ו**{כן לא תחשוב} **שאין הפרש בין קריעת ים סוף למשה וליוצאי מצרים**[ו] **-**

Reeds [performed on behalf] of Moses and those who left Egypt[1] or the crossing of the Jordan River [performed on behalf] of Elisha and Elijah,[2] and another instance [of a miraculous event found in the teachings of the Sages].[3]

[For without this approach], all these [faulty conclusions] would be necessary [outcomes] when reading these [exegeses] literally or accepting them at face value, [without proper analysis].

[In all honesty] it would have sufficed to [simply] instruct you [to be aware] that there exist exegeses and narratives which contain hidden matters that go beyond their literal context. Even more so [it would have sufficed to consider] what my father, of blessed memory, [has already] revealed in his books,[4] if it were not for my great desire to further explain [these matters] to you, and provide instances which

1 Exodus 14:21

2 II Kings 8:14

3 See, for example, *Ḥulin* 7a:

> **Rabbi Pineḥas ben Ya'ir was travelling to** engage in the **redemption of captives,** and **he encountered the River Ginai. He said to it** [the river], **"Ginai, part your waters for me, and I will pass through you."** The river **said to him, "You are going to perform the will of your Maker, and I am going to perform the will of my Maker,** that is to say: to flow in my path. With regard to **you,** it is **uncertain** whether you will **perform** His will successfully, **and** it is **uncertain** whether **you** will **not perform** His will successfully. **I,** however, will **certainly perform** His will successfully." Rabbi Pineḥas ben Ya'ir **said to him** [the river], "If **you do not part, I** shall **decree upon you that water will never flow through you."** The river **parted for him.**
>
> **A certain man was carrying wheat** for the preparation of *maṣa* **for Passover.** Rabbi Pineḥas ben Ya'ir **said to him** [the river], **"Part** your waters **for that** person **too, for he is engaged in** the performance of **a *miṣva.*"** The river **parted for him. A certain Arab was accompanying them.** Rabbi Pineḥas ben Ya'ir **said to him** [the river], **"Part** your waters **for that** person **too, so that he will not say, 'Is this** what **one does for those who accompany?'"** The river **parted for him.**
>
> **Rav Yosef said, "How much greater is this man,** Rabbi Pineḥas ben Ya'ir, **than Moses and the six hundred thousand** who left Egypt, **as there,** at the Sea of Reeds, the waters parted **one time, and here,** the waters parted **three times."** [The Gemara asks:] **And perhaps here too,** the waters parted **one time,** and the river began to flow again only after all three had passed? [The Gemara answers]: **Rather,** this man was as great **as Moses and the six hundred thousand** who left Egypt.

4 There exist countless examples of non-literal interpretation throughout the writings of the HaRaMBa"M. See, for example, his approach to the Messianic era and the World to Come in *The Laws of Repentance*, ch. 8, or in his introduction to *Pereq Ḥeleq*.

ובין צליחת הירדן לאלישע ולאליהו[7] - או {בקיעת ים אחר} לאחד זולת אלו.

ו{מאידך}, כל זה תתחייב כשתקח אותם הדרשות על פי פשוטן, או על פי הנראה מהם לכתחלה בעיון הראשון.

ו{באמת} די היה בנו להורות לך שיש מדרשות ומעשיות שיש להם ענין פנימי נסתר חוץ מהענין החיצוני הנראה - וכ"ש ב{הצטרפותן אל} מה שגילה אבא מרי ז"ל בחיבוריו מזה - לולי כי חפצי ורצוני להוסיפך ביאור ולהודיעך מעשים {=דוגמאות}

are categorised according to their subject matter – which I will soon categorise, along with examples which I will provide to you in this chapter.[1]

But [first and foremost,] I saw it proper to preface with the following introduction.

◆◆◆

1 As noted above, this chapter is from his magnum opus, *Kifāyat al-ʿĀbidīn* (*HaMaspiq LeỌvde Hashem*).

בחלוק עניניהם שאני מחלק לך בקרוב, ובמשלים {ש}אמשול לך בזה הפרק. וראיתי להקדים תחילה הקדמה זו.

◆◆◆

Chapter 2

Conviction and proper perception in matters of aggadah

2:1 – Introduction

Know, for it is your duty to know, that anyone who wishes to uphold a known theory and admire its author by [blindly] accepting it without proper analysis or verification of its truth, is [considered to possess] a deficient character trait. This [mode of conduct] is forbidden according to the way of the Torah, and is not an intelligent approach. It is intellectually dishonest because it entails deficiency and inadequacy in the contemplation of essential convictions,[1] and it is forbidden according to the ways of the Torah because it deviates from the way of truth and from the straight line [meaning: that which is morally binding].[2] [For] God states, *"do not favour the poor*

1 Although the original Arabic text of this chapter is no longer extant, we can see from the surviving original Arabic fragments of the middle third of this work that the word which has been translated into Hebrew as *emuna* is *i'tiqad* in Arabic. There is much misunderstanding today concerning both terms. The root of the Hebrew word *emuna* lies in Biblical and Rabbinic literature, where it connotes faithfulness, trust, reliance, and acceptance. Later philosophers use this terminology with additional meanings. Due to the lack of technical philosophical terms in Hebrew, *emuna* was first used in rendering the Arabic term *i'tiqad*, used by Rabbenu Avraham in this sentence, and by his father HaRaMBa"M (See, for example, *Guide* 1:50), and it refers to reason-based conviction. The word *emuna* continued to be used in this original sense in Jewish philosophical literature through the thirteenth and fourteenth centuries as many scientific works were transmitted to the West and translated from Arabic to Hebrew. Later, as scholasticism began to influence Jewish thought, *emuna* took on the meaning of 'faith' in the sense of blind acceptance, authority-based assent, or *fides*. For a Rabbinic analysis, see Rabbi Yosef Qafiḥ, *Ketavim*, II, p. 594. For an academic analysis, see Charles H. Manekin, *Hebrew Philosophy in the Fourteenth and Fifteenth Centuries: an Overview*, p. 353. For an example of the term *emuna* used by ḤaZa"L in its original connotations, see *Shabbat* 31a. For an example of the term *emuna* used in Scripture, see Exodus 17:12, Psalms 92:23, Isaiah 33:16, and Jeremiah 15:18, among others.

2 The Torah attributes the character trait of truth to God and emphasises the pursuit of truth for man. To believe in something without proper investigation would be in contradiction to the virtue of truth.

פרק ב

האמונה וההבחנה השכלית בדברי אגדה

ב:א - הקדמה

ד ע, כי אתה חייב לדעת, כל מי שירצה להעמיד דעת ידועה, ולישא פני אומרה ולקבל דעתו בלי עיון והבטה לענין אותו דעת אם {ה}אמת אִתָּהּ אם לא, שזה מן הדעות הרעות, והוא נאסר מדרך התורה, וגם {אינו} מדרך השכל. אינו מדרך השכל - מפני שהוא מחייב גרעון וחסרון בהתבוננות {ב}מה ש{מ} צריך {האדם} להאמין בו. ו{נאסר} מדרך התורה - מפני שנוטה מדרך האמת ונוטה מעל קו הישר. {הרי} אמר הש"ית לא תשא פני דל ולא תהדר פני

nor show deference to the great; judge your people fairly," and *"you shall not be partial in judgment."*[1]

There is no difference between the acceptance of a certain theory without proof, or believing and admiring its author; as if the truth is unquestionably with him due to his great stature, such as Heman, Khalkhol, and Darda̩.[2] For none of this is [intellectually] acceptable and it is forbidden [according to the ways of the Torah].[3]

According to this preface, we can deduce that we are not bound to the Talmudic Sages because of their greatness and wisdom, or because of their expertise in explaining the Torah with its fine details, or because of the truth of their statements when elucidating the general and specific components [of the Torah], [that we must] answer for them and maintain their views regarding all they say concerning medicine, science, or astronomy.[4] [We are not required] to say that the truth is with them [in these matters]

1 Leviticus 19:15; Deuteronomy 1:17. A judge must be impartial and assess each claim on its own merit, regardless of who said it. Similarly, an ordinary person must judge a certain theory on its own merit, regardless of who said it.

2 I Kings 5:11. Heman, Khalkhol, and Darda̩ were the famous wise children of Maḥol who were outsmarted by King Solomon.

3 This is the logical fallacy of "appeal to authority."

4 Rabbenu Avraham's approach is congruent with the Geonic–Andalusian tradition, which regards statements of the Sages on medicine, science, or astronomy to be non-binding since they were not received through direct tradition.

Regarding medicine, Rav Sherira Gaon (906–1006, academy of Pumbedita, Babylonia) writes:

> We must inform you that our Sages were not physicians. They may mention medical matters which they noticed here and there in their time, but these are not meant to be a *miṣva*. Therefore you should not rely on these cures and you should not practice them at all unless each item has been carefully investigated by medical experts who are certain that this procedure will do no harm and will cause no danger [to the patient]. This is what our ancestors have taught us, that none of these cures should be practiced, unless it is a known remedy and the one who uses it knows that it can cause no harm. (*Oṣar HaGeonim*, *Giṭin* 68, #376) [translation by Rabbi Aryeh Carmell OBM]

Regarding astrology, HaRaMBa"M writes:

> You must, however, not expect that everything our Sages say regarding astronomical matters should agree with observation, for mathematics were not fully developed in those days, and their statements were not based on the authority of the Prophets, but on the

גדול בצדק תשפוט עמיתך,[ט] ואמר **לא תכירו פנים במשפט וגו'.**[י]

ואין הפרש בין קבלת אותו דעת להעמידה בלא ראיה, או בין שנאמין לאומרה ונשא לו פנים ונטעון לו כי האמת אתו בלי ספק מפני שהוא אדם גדול {כ}הימן וכלכל ודרדע,[י] {מפני} שכל זה אינו ראוי {מדרך השכל}, **ואסור** {מדרך התורה}.

ו{יוצא לנו} לפי הקדמה זו {ש}לא נתחייב מפני גודל מעלת חכמי התלמוד וחכמתם, ו{מפני} שלימות תכונתם בפירוש התורה ובדקדוקיה, ו{מפני} יושר אמריהם בביאור כלליה ופרטיה, שנטעון להם ונעמיד דעתם בכל אמריהם {אפילו} ברפואות ובחכמת הטבע והתכונה, ולומר האמת

in the same way in which we believe them regarding their explanations of the Torah, since [only] this form of wisdom [that is to say: exposition of the Torah] is their mastery, and to them was given the jurisdiction to instruct people in it, as the verse states *According to the Torah which they shall teach you [...you shall act...]*[1, 2]

One can observe the Sages' [manifestation of this attitude] in [their reaction to] statements which were not logically sound in their eyes, to which they would respond, "By God, even if Joshua, son of Nun would have said it [to me directly], I would not have listened

knowledge which they either themselves possessed or derived from contemporary men of science. (*Guide* 3:14)

It is quite right that our Sages have abandoned their own theory: for speculative matters each one treats according to the results of his own study, and each one accepts that which appears to him established by proof. (*Guide* 2:8)

On the latter, Rabbi Shem Ṭov ben Yosef ben Shem Ṭov (1461-1489, Spain) comments: "Know that this teaching is the most valuable of all precious utensils, as many things will become clear as a result of it to those who want to enter the depths of Torah."

See also how HaRaMBa"M dealt with the Sages' belief regarding astrology:

I know that you may search and find sayings of some individual sages in the Talmud and *midrashim* whose words appear to maintain that at the moment of a man's birth, the stars will cause such and such to happen to him. Do not regard this as a difficulty, for it is not fitting for a man to abandon the prevailing law and raise once again the counterarguments and replies (that preceded its enactment). Similarly, it is not proper to abandon matters of reason that have already been verified by proofs, shake loose of them, and depend on the words of a single one of the sages from whom possibly the matter was hidden. (*Letter on Astrology*)

Rabbi Samson Raphael Hirsch, too, writes:

And if, as we see things today, these instances are considered fiction, can the Sages be blamed for ideas that were accepted by the naturalists of their times? And this is what really happened. These statements are to be found in the works of Pliny, who lived in Rome at the time the Second Temple was destroyed, and who collected in his books on nature all that was well known and accepted in his day. (*Trusting the Torah's Sages*)

1 Deuteronomy 17:11

2 See *Torah, Chazal & Science* (R. Meiselman, p. 110), who critiques this paragraph (as part of his novel attempt to prove that a portion of this work is a forgery) by saying:

This seems to indicate that *CḤaZa"L* have no authority at all outside of *halachah* and Scriptural interpretation. If this rendering is correct, it puts the author at odds with all other *Rishonim*. It is possible, however, that there is some inexactitude in the translation and that he was referring only to those instances in which *CḤaZa"L*'s *mesorah* was incomplete and

אתם {בזה} כאשר נאמין אותם בפירוש התורה שתכלית חכמתה בידם, ולהם נמסרה להורתה לבני אדם, כענין שנאמר **על פי התורה אשר יורוך וגו'**.[ק]

אתה רואה {שמנהג} החכמים ז"ל במה שלא נתברר להם מדרך סברתם ומשאם ומתנם {שהם} אומרים **'האלהים, אילו אמרה יהושע בן נון לא ציתנא**

to him."[1] That is to say: "I would not believe him, even though he is a

they were unable to extract the needed information through the methodologies of the *Torah shebe'al Peh.*

He then (p. 111) attempts to prove from *Hilkhot Qiddush HaḤodesh* that HaRaMBa"M did not fully follow this approach:

> There [*Qiddush HaḤodesh* 17:24] HaRaMBa"M writes that the reasons for the calculations used in the establishment of the calendar must be learned from the books of the Greeks because those composed by the Jews in the days of the Prophets were lost. His intention is clear – the calculations were not forgotten, only the reasons for them.
>
> This is evident from numerous statements throughout the laws of *Kiddush HaḤodesh.* To cite just a few, in 11:1 HaRaMBa"M writes that as long as the Sanhedrin was functioning, they were able to determine precisely when the moon would be visible. A few *halachos* later (11:4), he writes that these calculations compromise the *Sod HaIbur* – the "Secret of Intercalation" which was known to the great scholars, who would pass it on only to the worthy. In a later chapter (18:8) he states explicitly that a certain detail of the calendrical calculations was part of a received tradition going back to Moshe *Rabbeinu.*
>
> Clearly then HaRaMBa"M never meant that *CḤaZa"L* had no reliable traditions regarding the physical world. All he meant was that some information had been lost. Regarding that information, *CḤaZa"L* were forced to rely upon the wisdom of the gentiles or upon tentative understandings. Apparently in HaRaMBa"M's view, the particular dicta he had in mind in the *Moreh* were just such tentative statements made in areas in which the passage *Mesorah* had been lost.

From all the aforementioned sources cited by Rabbi Meiselman, only once does HaRaMBa"M actually mention that there existed an unbroken tradition:

> Rather the tradition that was in the hand of the Sages – *one man from the mouth of another, from the mouth of Moses, our teacher* – is thus: That at a time when the moon is not seen at the beginning of [several] months – one month after the other – the court sets a [full] month of thirty days and a lacking month of twenty-nine days. (*Hilkhot Qiddush HaḤodesh* 18:8)

Nevertheless, this law has nothing to do with astronomical phenomena or the "physical world," but rather with halakhic constructs. Though HaRaMBa"M does mention that the *Bet Din* knew exactly when the moon would appear (ibid., 11:1), or that the Secret of Intercalation was privately revealed to certain individuals (compare *Hilkhot Yesodei haTorah* 4:11), or that the tribe of Yissakhar were experts in this field (ibid., 17:24), nowhere do we see that HaRaMBa"M claims that they were infallible due to a direct tradition from Sinai.

Furthermore, HaRaMBa"M (end of ibid., 17:24) clearly states that the intricacies of the sanctification of the month are dependent on scientific evidence, which is accepted regardless of whom it is learned from:

> Since all these rules have been established by sound and clear proofs, free from any flaw and irrefutable, we need not be concerned about the identity of their authors, whether they were Hebrew Prophets or gentile sages. For when we have to do with rules and propositions which have been demonstrated by good reasons and have been verified to be true by sound and flawless proofs, we do not need to rely upon the author who has discovered them or has transmitted them, but on his demonstrated proofs and verified reasoning.

1 *Ḥulin* 124a

ליהי[ט] - כלומר 'לא הייתי מאמין לו, ואע"פ שהוא

Prophet, since it is not within his ability to properly represent the matter according to logical deduction and methods of Talmudic exposition."[1]

No further claim is needed, as it is a sufficient enough proof [to note] that we find statements of theirs that are neither proven nor verified; for

1 R. Meiselman (ibid.) calls this passage into question as well:

> As the author interprets it (*Hullin* 124a), the implication is that when logic is involved, there can be no appeal to authority - even in matters of *halachah*! In other words, if I am convinced logically, I must not accept anyone else's word, even if he belongs to an earlier period - even if he is *Moshe Rabbeinu's* protégé and successor Yehoshua bin Nun. (p. 112)

He then notes how Rabbenu Avraham's interpretation of this statement conflicts with that of HaRaMBa"M:

> In his *Peirush HaMishnayos* he explains it to mean that prophecy plays no role in establishing the *halachah*. Hence it is a statement about the halachic process in specific, not about the establishment of truths in general. In fact, in an epistle to the people of Marseilles (Montpelier) on the topic of astrology, HaRaMBa"M identifies three legitimate grounds for believing a proposition demonstration: (1) logical demonstration (2) the evidence of the senses; and (3) receipt from an accepted authority such as a prophet or righteous man. From this encapsulation it is clear that HaRaMBa"M, in contrast to the author of the *Maamar*, does consider receipt from an authoritative personality as valid grounds for conviction. This disagreement, compounded by their divergent interpretations of the Gemara, certainly calls into question the ascription of this discussion to Rabbeinu Avraham. (112-113)

It is difficult to comprehend R. Meiselman's proof from the epistle, for even according to HaRaMBa"M's explanation of the statement in his *Commentary to the Mishna*, anything stated by Joshua would nevertheless be a "receipt from an authoritative personality" (the third of HaRaMBa"M's legitimate grounds for relying on a statement), as Joshua was both a Prophet and righteous man.

Obviously HaRaMBa"Ms' three categories of legitimate grounds for reliance are not unequivocal and indisputable, rather he is advising that "it is improper for a man to [initially] accept as trustworthy anything other than one of these three things." (*Letter to the Community of Marseille*). Nevertheless, one who further investigates a matter and has reason to believe otherwise surely retains the right to disagree.

Furthermore, although HaRaMBa"M applied the passage in *Ḥulin* to the halakhic process *vis a vis* prophecy, Rabbenu Avraham's application of it to general truth stems from the same source, as there is no monopoly when it comes to reason, whether one is a prophet or not. Even regarding decrees of the *Bet Din*, HaRaMBa"M writes (*Hilkhot Mamrim* 2:1):

> When the Great *Bet Din* used one of the principles of exegesis to derive a law through their perception of the matter and adjudicated a case accordingly, and afterwards a later court arose and perceived another rationale which would revoke

נביא, כיון שאין בידו יכולת להודיע הענין בכוונה מדרך הסברא והמשא והמתן והדרכים שבהם ניתן התלמוד להדרש.'

ודי בזה ראיה ומופת, ולא נטעון להם עוד, כיון שאנחנו מוצאים להם אמרים {=מאמרים} שלא

example, their statements regarding medicine, particularly the [potency of] the *even tequma* (preservation-stone), which they said prevents miscarriages, have not been proven.[1]

Likewise, [this is the case] regarding the many matters discussed in [chapter] *Shemona Sheraṣim*, as well as in other places,

the previous ruling, the [later *Bet Din*] may revoke it and rule according to their perception.

Similarly, regarding the ability of post-Talmudic authorities to dispute their post-Talmudic predecessors, HaRaMBa"M writes (*Mishne Torah, Introduction*):

> If one of the Geonim interpreted a law in a certain way, and afterwards a later court perceived that way as an incorrect understanding of the Gemara, the first opinion need not be adhered to. Rather, whichever position appears to be correct – whether first or last – is accepted.

The only reason HaRaMBa"M does not allow post-Talmudic authorities to dispute rulings of Talmudic (or earlier) authorities is due to the lack of a national consensus, as he writes (ibid.): "However, regarding everything in the Babylonian Talmud, all of Israel is obligated to follow its [rulings]...since everything in the Talmud was agreed upon by all of Israel."

Nevertheless, as mentioned above, due to technical halakhic considerations, one is bound to the rulings of the *Bet Din* until a later *Bet Din* rescinds the former's rulings. We thus see that, even in matters of *halakha*, there are instances where later authorities can argue, even with someone who belongs to an earlier period.

Moreover, unlike R. Meiselman's understanding (p. 114), Rabbenu Avraham's statement here is not granting the ability to dispute a direct tradition from Moses, as he clearly writes later: "If it be a tradition then we must accept it, but if it be an inference [based on your own reasoning] we have [meaning: can accept] a refutation."

1 *Shabbat* 66b. As the Sages taught in a *beraita*:

> One may go out with a preservation-stone, which prevents miscarriages, on the Sabbath. They said in the name of Ribbi Meir that one may go out even with the counterweight of a preservation-stone [that is to say: a stone or another object that was weighed against and found equivalent to the weight of the preservation stone, which is also effective]. This leniency applies not only to a woman who miscarried in the past and is concerned that she may miscarry again; rather, it applies even to a woman who never miscarried and is concerned lest she miscarry for the first time. It applies not only to a woman who is aware that she is pregnant; rather, it applies even if a woman suspects that she may become pregnant and miscarry.

HaRaMBa"M (*Hilkhot Shabbat*) codifies this:

> A woman may go out with a preservation-stone or the counterweight of a preservation-stone which was weighed with the intent that it serve as a remedy. And not only a

נתאמתו ולא נתקיימו, כגון דברי הרפואות וכענין אבן תקומה שאמרו' שמונע להפיל הנפלים, שלא נתאמת {ענין זה}.

וכיוצא בזה ענינים רבים שדברו במס' שבת ב {פרק} שמונה שרצים[יא] - ובמקומות אחרות - דברים שבחנו

all of which were items examined by experts during their time, whom the Sages relied on; [in our time, however,] neither a

pregnant woman, but even other women lest she become pregnant and have a miscarriage. (19:14)

From here, too, R. Meiselman calls the authenticity of this passage into question:

> The author of this part of the *Ma'amar*, by contrast [to HaRaMBa"M], says that there is no evidence that an even tekumah is effective and that we may disregard *Chazal's* attestation to the contrary on this account. (p. 116)

It is difficult to comprehend R. Meiselmans' stance, for HaRaMBa"M explains the nature of similar items (*Guide* III, 37:4):

> Do not ask yourself why [the Rabbis] permitted [one to carry, on the Sabbath] a nail from a crucifixion or a fox's tooth, for these were thought (חשבו) to be effective during that time period and were thus used for medical reasons....For anything confirmed by experience is permitted for therapeutic purposes.

Rabbi Yosef Qafiḥ comments that the original Arabic word for "thought" (חשבו) was "ט'ן," which means a false or mistaken conviction. There is no reason why HaRaMBa"M would not state the same about the preservation stone. Moreover, although he codified the permissibility of carrying the preservation stone in *Mishne Torah* (along with the nail from a crucifixion and a fox's tooth), the RaDBa"Z explains that the sages permitted certified *segula* treatments when no Torah prohibition is transgressed (*Responsa of RaDBa"Z*, V, 1436): "For anything that a person carries on the Sabbath for medicinal reasons is worn, and [thus] no Sabbath prohibition is transgressed." (See Rabbenu Ḥananel, *Arukh*, and Meiri who explain that the preservation-stone would be worn "תלויה על אישה" – "hung on a woman," though RaSH"I writes "אבן שנושאות אותה" – "that stone which they carry.")

Accordingly, though Rabbenu Avraham states that the Sages were incorrect in their conviction in the efficacy of the preservation-stone, there is no indication that he would dispute his father's decision in *Mishne Torah*, especially in light of its codification in the Tannaitic era.

Even if one were to reject the explanation of the RaDBa"Z in cases where the science of the Sages differs from modern medicine, the halakhic decisions of the *Bet Din HaGadol* would nevertheless still be binding, as HaRaMBa"M writes (*Hilkhot Sheḥiṭa* 10:12–13):

> One may not add to this list of causes of *ṭerefa*, for in the case of any other [defect that] occurs in an animal, beast, or bird, beyond those which the Sages of former generations have enumerated, and to which the *Batei Din* of Israel have agreed, it is possible for the animal to live, even if our own medical knowledge assures us that it cannot eventually survive.
>
> Similarly, [those defects] which the Sages have enumerated and have said that they render the animal *ṭerefa*, even though it is seen through our own medical knowledge that some of them are not fatal and that the animal can still survive, one must go only by what the Sages have enumerated, as it is said, "*You shall act in accordance with the instructions given to you.*" (Deuteronomy 17:11).

See Rab Yiṣḥaq HaLevi Herzog (*Hekhal Yiṣḥaq, Oraḥ Ḥayim* 29) who applies this approach to the Sages' belief that lice spontaneously generate, leading to their

אותם הבוחנים {בזמנם} **ונשמעו ביניהם וסמכו הם**
{=החכמים ז"ל} **עליהם, ו**{אמנם כיום} **לא יודה על**

reliable doctor nor an intelligent person would admit to their truth.[1]

And know that it is unnecessary to apply the same methodology to [other teachings of the Sages] because of what we just mentioned [regarding the rejection of the preservation stone and the like]. [For example, regarding] what they stated "if you are hungry, eat; if you are thirsty, drink; if your pot is cooked, pour it out while it is still hot."[2] [One need not reject this teaching because of what we mentioned] for this teaching is a fundamental of health, as has been verified through experiment and doctors' remedies. [As this teaching] is stating that one should not eat until hungry, nor drink until thirsty, and when thirsty, one should not delay to drink, and once the food is digested in one's stomach, one should not delay to relieve oneself if one feels the urge.[3]

Conversely, we must not claim that since Aristotle was the greatest of philosophers and because he established indisputable facts about the

---

permissive ruling to kill them on the Sabbath:

> It is permissible to kill a louse on Shabbat, since it does not reproduce, as explained in tractate *Shabbat* 107... Although modern science, as far as I know, does not acknowledge the existence of spontaneous generation, for halakhic purposes we have nothing other than the words of the Sages.

Rabbi Moshe Shmuel Glasner (introduction to *Dor Revi'i* on *Ḥulin*) notes similarly:

> Now in truth, the scientific consensus today is that there is no insect that does not procreate by means of eggs. Nevertheless, we shall not overturn the law, even in the name of stringency, against the ruling and consensus of our Sages...

1 For an alternative approach, see the Meiri (*Bet HaBeḥira, Shabbat* 67a) who explains that these remedies and incantations were exclusive to uneducated people and were permitted due to the power of their placebo effect.

2 *Berakhot* 62b. As with many Talmudic passages that Rabbenu Avraham cites, his text will vary from that found in the standard Vilna edition: "Until (עד) you are hungry, eat; until you are thirsty, drink; until your pot boils, pour it out."

3 See RaSH"I (*Berakhot* 62b) explains that food is only beneficial when one has an appetite and thus one should not delay. (Perhaps he means that food is digested more effectively when one is hungry.) Like Rabbenu Avraham, HaRaMBa"M (*Hilkhot Deọt* 4:1) codifies that one should not eat or drink until hungry or thirsty. However, Rabbenu Avraham does add additional instruction: "and when thirsty, one should not delay to drink" (which is how R. Hai Gaon explains the Gemara; see *Ạrukh*, entry כפן).

אמיתת {ם אחר ה}**עיון** {לא} **רופא אמיתי ולא שכלן.**

ודע כי {גם} **לא יתחייב בעבור מה שאמרנו** {ההיפך מזה, כגון} **שיהא** {אדם אומר ב}**מה שאמרו חז"ל אי כפנת אכול אי צחית שתה אי בשל קדרך שדי במכמנא,'**[ג] **הדברים שאמרנו** {באבן תקומה וכיוצא בה}**. כי זה המאמר הוא עיקר הבריאות כאשר אמתוהו הבחינה ורפואות הרופאים, ר"ל שלא יאכל אדם עד שירעב, ושלא ישתה עד שיצמא, וכשיצמא שלא יאחר לשתות, וכשיתעכל המזון במיעיו שישליכנו ולא יאחרנו,** {ו}**שאם צריך לנקביו שלא ישהה אותם.**

וכן אין לנו לטעון לאריסטו ולומר הואיל ואדון חכמי הפילוסופים הוא והקים מופתים אמיתיים

existence of God, may He be blessed, as well as other true matters, that he arrived at the truth regarding the eternal existence of the world, or [accept his view on] the Creator's lack of knowledge [regarding] [minute] details, or [his view on] other similar matters.[1] [On the other hand], we must not [be quick] to reject him by stating that due to his errors in certain opinions he must therefore have erred in all his statements. Rather, it is our duty – and the duty of every intelligent and wise person – to assess each opinion and statement, in whatever manner it must be analysed, and uphold that which is worth upholding, and do away with anything unworthy.[2] [We must also] refrain from ruling [on cases] which cannot be decided one way or the other.

[It is proper to practice this method of thinking for all matters,] regardless of who propounds it, as we see in the [words of] Sages, of blessed memory, who said "If it [the law] be a tradition, we accept it, but if it be an inference [based on your own reasoning], there is [that is to say: there can be] a refutation."[3] Similarly, in instances

1 Similarly, HaRaMBa"M writes (*Guide* 2:25):

> If we were to accept the Eternity of the Universe as taught by Aristotle, that everything in the Universe is the result of fixed laws, that Nature does not change, and that there is nothing supernatural, we should necessarily be in opposition to the foundation of our religion, we should disbelieve all miracles and signs, and certainly reject all hopes and fears derived from Scripture, unless the miracles are also explained figuratively. The Allegorists amongst the Mohammedans have done this, and have thereby arrived at absurd conclusions.

2 This is reminiscent of HaRaMBa"M's statement in his introduction to *Shemona Peraqim*:

> Know, however, that the ideas presented in these chapters and in the following commentary are not of my own invention; neither did I think out the explanations contained therein, but I have gleaned them from the words of the wise occurring in the *Midrashim*, in the Talmud, and in other of their works, as well as from the words of the philosophers, ancient and recent, and also from the works of various authors, as one should accept the truth from whoever says it.

However, due to his awareness of the individual's difficulty in comprehending this concept, he chose to omit the names of the sources:

> Sometimes, too, the mention of the name of the authority drawn upon might lead one who lacks insight to believe that the statement quoted is faulty and wrong, because he does not understand it. Therefore, I prefer not to mention the authority, for my intention is only to be of service to the reader, and to elucidate for him the thoughts hidden in this tractate.

3 *Yevamot* 76b, *Keritut* 15b. Rabbenu Avraham uses a similar quote in his commentary to the Torah in the context of the right to dispute certain midrashic interpretations.

על מציאות הבורא ית' - וכיוצא בזה מהדברים אמיתיים שבאו במופת ופגעו דרך האמת - כי כן מצא האמת באמונת קדמות העולם, ושאין הבורא ית' יודע הפרטים וכיוצא בזה. ו{מאידך, גם} לא {נתחייבנו} להכזיבו ולומר הואיל וטעה באמונת אלו, כי כן טעה בכל אמריו. אבל יש לנו ולכל נבון וחכם להתבונן כל דיעה וכל מאמר, על דרך שיש להתבונן אותה, ולאמת ולקיים מה שראוי לקיים, ולבטל מה שראוי לבטלו. ו{כן עלינו} לעמוד מלפסוק הדין במה שלא הוכרע {בו כצד} האחד משני הפכים.

{וכן ראוי לעשות בכל דבר ודבר} - אמרו מי שאמרו, כאשר אנו רואים אותם ז"ל {נוהגים, כמו} שאמרו אם הלכה נקבל ואם לדין יש תשובה.[יג] וכן הם

where a case could not be resolved, they ceased the discussion with "*tequ*" ("let it remain unsolved"). [Similarly,] they would retract [their opinions] in light of an alternative deemed to be true, as we often find their statement "*hadar beh Rav Peloni*" ("Rav [X] retracted"),[1] or "the academy of Hillel retracted and decided in accordance with the academy of Shammai."[2]

Furthermore, out of their [unashamed] admission to the truth, and their love for acting justly, they stated, "Rava placed an interpreter before him [in order to tell the public that he had erred], and [publicly] said 'the statements I made before you are my error.'"[3]

Matters such as this and those similar[4] should not be understood and observed because of their authors' [general] profound advice and wisdom, but because of the undisputed evidence supporting them. And so did my father and teacher, of blessed memory, state in the *Guide*.[5] This

See his comments on Genesis 46:26 and Exodus 2:1.

1 *Shabbat* 40a

2 *Ẹduyot* 1:12, *Yevamot* 116b. Unlike the leaders or authorities of many religions - who are perceived (and perceive themselves) as infallible - the Sages were very open to admit to their mistakes. Rabbenu Avraham writes similarly in a collection of his responsa:

> For this is the action of faithful men, who engage in Torah for its own sake, meaning the seeking of truth, not triumph. For no shame inhabits a sage who retracts from an error that has happened to him or from a mistake [made] due to the truth being hidden from him. It is, rather, to the contrary, [for] he receives a reward from God, may He be exalted, for retraction from his error after it has been revealed to him that he was mistaken... This is apparent from the actions of the great Sages of Israel, of blessed memory, whose chronicles were recorded so that men of faith would learn morals from the pleasantness of their actions. (*Teshuvot Rabbenu Avraham ben HaRaMB"AM*, ed. Freiman, Goitein, 82, p. 108)

3 *Bava Batra* 127a; *Zevaḥim* 94b, *Nida* 68a. This is reminiscent of Rabbenu Avraham's testimony regarding his father:

> והרי תמיד ראינוהו ז"ל בבירור מסכים אל הקטן שבתלמידיו, לגבי האמת, למרות עושר לימודו שלא עמד בניגוד למופלגות דתו.
>
> We always clearly saw [my father], of blessed memory, concurring with [even the] smallest of his students regarding the truth, for notwithstanding his wealth of knowledge, he would never stand against those who would argue on his opinion. (*HaMaspiq LeỌvde HaShem, Kitab Kifāyat al-'Ābidīn*, ed. and trans. N. Dana, page 71, Bar Ilan University, 1989.)

4 Rabbenu Avraham seems to be giving a recap of his previous statements.

5 Rabbenu Avraham does not specify the place (in the *Guide*) to which he is referring. R.

עושים במה שלא הוכרע האחד משני הפכין, שמעמידים אותו באמרם בו **תיקו.**[י] ו{כן} **חוזרים** להם מדעת שנתאמת להם, כאמרם בהרבה מקומות הדר ביה ר' **פלוני,**[טו] {או} **חזרו בית הלל להורות כדברי בית שמאי.**[טז]

וגדול מזה (בהוראתם) [בהודאתם] על האמת ואהבתם דרך המשפט אמרו **אוקי רבא אמורא עליה ודרש ואמר דברים שאמרתי בפניכם טעות הם בידי.**[יז]

ועניינים אלו וכיוצא בהם אין להבינם ולהתבונן בהם מפני אומרם שהיה גדול העצה והחכמה, אלא מפני הראיות והמופתים שיש עליהם. וכן אמר אבא

is clear and easily understood by anyone who turns from his physical desire.[1]

2:2 – Evidence of the Sages' Great Regard for the Characteristic of Searching for Truth

I saw it fitting to bring a teaching of our Sages, of blessed memory, and explain it to you so that the Sages' love of truth and acceptance of it – irrespective of who said it – shall settle and gain credence in your mind. They, of blessed memory, stated in *Pesaḥim*:[2]

> **Our Sages taught, the Sages of Israel state that the** ***galgal***[3] **is stationary, and the** ***mazalot***[4] **revolve** within the sphere, **and the wise men of the gentile nations state that the** ***galgal*** **revolves and the** ***mazalot*** **are stationary. Ribbi** Yehudah HaNasi **stated,** "There exists **a refutation to their words, for we have never found** the constellation of ***Agala*** (Ursa Major) **in the south and** ***Aqrav*** (Scorpio) **in the north."**[5]
>
> **Rav Aḥa bar Yaaqov rejected this,** stating **"Perhaps it is like the steel** socket **of a mill,**[6] **or like the pivot of a door.**[7]**"**[8]

Moshe Maimon (*Ma'amar Al HaDerashot veAl HaAggadot*, p.32) suggests *Guide* II, 15: "For a truth, once established by proof, does not gain force or certainty by the consent of all scholars, nor does its validity decrease or weaken by the dissent of the general population."

1 Physical desire can cause one to accept certain opinions that inhibit one from arriving at truth. As HaRaMBa"M warns (*Guide* I, 50):

> When your desires and habits are removed, and when you conquer your reason, and study what I am going to say in the chapters which follow on the rejection of the attributes; you will then be fully convinced of what we have said.

2 94b

3 the celestial sphere of the zodiac wherein the stars move

4 the constellations

5 This indicates that the constellations themselves revolve in place, not the celestial sphere as a whole. For if the celestial sphere moved as a whole, the constellations would not always remain in the same positions in respect to the cardinal directions.

6 which remains stationary while the stones of the mill revolve around it

7 which remains stationary while the door makes wide turns around it

8 Meaning: perhaps the constellations are stationary within a sphere, and there exists

מרי ז"ל במורה, והוא דבר מבואר וענין קל בעיני כל נוטה מעל תאות גופו.

ב:ב - ראיות על הפלגת מדת ביקוש האמת של חז"ל

וראיתי להביא כאן מאמר שאמרו ז"ל, ואבארנו לך כדי שיתיישב ויתקבל בדעתך אהבתם {את} האמת והודאתם עליו - אמרו מי שאמרו. אמרו ז"ל בגמ' פסחים[יח] ת"ר חכמי ישראל אומרים גלגל קבוע ומזלות חוזרין [וכו' עד] [וחכמי אומות העולם אומרים גלגל חוזר ומזלות קבועין, אמר רבי תשובה לדבריהם מעולם לא מצינו עגלה בדרום ועקרב בצפון, מתקיף לה רב אחא בר יעקב ודילמא כבוצינא דריחיא אי נמי כצינורא דדשא.

The Sages of Israel state that during the day, the sun travels underneath the firmament, and at night above the firmament.[1] However, the wise men of the gentile nations state that during the day, the sun travels underneath the firmament, and at night underneath the Earth.[2] Ribbi Yehudah HaNasi **stated, "Their words appear more accurate, as we see that during the day, the springs are cold, while at night they are hot."[3]**

Now, pay heed to the explanation of this teaching. It stated that the opinion of the Sages of Israel is that the celestial sphere is stationary, unmoving, and motionless, while the stars and constellations shift and move.[4] [However, the opinion of] the wise men of the gentile nations is that the celestial sphere moves and shifts, while the stars and constellations are stationary, like well-fastened nails, and only move as a result of the celestial sphere's movement, not their own.[5]

The opinion of the wise men of the gentile nations can be refuted by proving that the celestial sphere is [actually] stationary, [due to the fact that] we see the small constellations on the left and right [of the night sky] [remaining in their respective positions consistently,] without the left moving to the right nor the right moving to the left, rather they

an outer sphere within which the sun revolves around all the constellations. Thus, the constellations would remain in the same positions in respect to the cardinal directions.

1 In Biblical cosmology, the firmament is a solid dome, created on the second day of Creation, which divided the first waters into upper and lower sections so that the earth's dry land could appear. Accordingly, while the sun travels underneath the firmament it would be visible and while it travels above the firmament it would not. According to this approach, the sun would enter and exit daily through an opening in the firmament, always remaining above the earth.

2 Accordingly, the sun rotates around the Earth, always within the firmament.

3. The springs are warmed by the sun while it travels underneath the Earth.

4. The stars do not actually rotate around the world, but rather shift away and reappear.

5 HaRaMBa"M follows this approach:

> This Being is the God of the universe, Lord of the whole Earth, who guides the *galgal* with an infinite force, a force of perpetual motion; for the *galgal* revolves continuously, which would be impossible without someone causing it to revolve; and it is He, blessed is He, Who causes it to revolve without hand and without body. (*Mishne Torah, Yesodei haTorah* 1:5 [see also: 3:2-5])

חכמי ישראל אומרים ביום חמה מהלכת למטה מן הרקיע ובלילה למעלה מן הרקיע, וחכמי אומות העולם אומרים ביום חמה מהלכת למטה מן הרקיע ובלילה למטה מן הקרקע] אמר רבי נראים דבריהם שביום מעינות צוננין ובלילה מעינות רותחין.

ועתה, שמע פירוש המימרא, אמר {=התלמוד} שדעת חכמי ישראל {היא} שהגלגל קבוע ועומד ולא יתנדנד ולא יתנועע, והכוכבים והמזלות הם הנעים והנדים. ולחכמי אומות העולם שגלגל נע ונד והכוכבים והמזלות אין להם תנועה, אך הם כמסמרות נטועים, ונעים בתנועות הגלגל ולא מעצמם.

ויש להשיב על דעת חכמי אומות העולם ולומר {=ולהוכיח} שגלגל קבוע, שהרי אנו רואים מזלות הקטנים - השמאלי מהם והימיני - שלא ימצא לעולם השמאלי בימין ולא הימיני בשמאל, אלא

remain in their places and do not move from there. This is what our Rabbis, of blessed memory [Ribbi Yehudah HaNasi] meant in stating that *Agala* has never been seen in the south, nor *Aqrav* in the north.[1]

[However], this answer shall only refute the [opinion of the wise men of the] nations of the world if they assume that the movement of the celestial sphere is from the north to the south or from the south to the north. However, in the event that they are of the opinion that the upper celestial sphere moves from east to west, and that of the constellations moves from west to east, the refutation [of Ribbi Yehudah HaNasi] would not apply, and [thus] the dispute would remain.[2] For in stating that the [upper] celestial sphere's motion is from east to west and that of the constellations is from west to east, it results that *Agala* would always be situated in the north and *Aqrav* in the south, not moving from their positions, and thus the left would not be seen to the right nor the right to the left, as is apparent to one who understands this subject matter and the subject matter of astronomy.[3] For there is no doubt that the refutation of Ribbi [Yehudah HaNasi] was based on the assumption that they believed that the celestial sphere moved from north to south, [for only then] would his refutation "for we have never found..." be logical.[4]

Rav Aḥa raises a difficulty relating to this [Ribbi's] refutation, stating that "perhaps it is like the steel [socket] of a mill, or like the pivot of a door." Meaning, perhaps the celestial sphere moves in its entirety – [while] the network of constellations remains in place,

1 North is left, while south is right. For the assumption is that the onlooker is facing east. See *Targum Onqelos* to Genesis 13:9.

2 Meaning: not all celestial spheres rotate in the same direction, and therefore it is possible that *Agala* and *Aqrav* remain in their respective positions even if their celestial sphere is in motion.

3 As HaRaMBa"M explains:

> Each of the eight spheres which contain the planets and stars are themselves divided into many spheres, one above the other like the layers of an onion. Some of these spheres revolve from the west to the east, and some revolve from the east to the west, such as the ninth sphere, which revolves from the east to the west... (*Mishne Torah, Hilkhot Yesodei haTorah* 3:2)

4 Rabbenu Avraham is accepting the approach of the wise men of the gentile nations due to his own understanding of astronomy, while rejecting Ribbi Yehudah

עומדים במקומם ולא יזוזו משם. הוא שאמרו רז"ל {אמר רבי תשובה לדבריהם} **מעולם לא נראית עגלה בדרום, ולא עקרב בצפון.**

וזאת התשובה לא יתיישבו בה אומות העולם, אלא באמרם {=אא"כ היו אומרים} כי סבת הגלגל ותנועתו (הוא) [היא] מן הצפון לדרום או מן הדרום לצפון. אבל בהיותם סוברים כי תנועת הגלגל העליון (הוא) [היא] ממזרח למערב, וגלגל המזלות ממערב למזרח, נסתלקה התשובה ונשארה המחלוקת. כי באומרו כי תנועת הגלגל {העליון} שהיא ממזרח למערב, וגלגל המזלות ממערב למזרח, ימצא כי {לעולם} עגלה בצפון ועקרב בדרום ולא יזוזו ממקומם, ולא יראה השמאלי ימיני ולא הימיני שמאלי - כאשר נודע למי שהבינו בזה הענין והבין בענין התכונה. כי אין ספק כי רבי בהשיבו עליהם - שחשב כי סברתם היתה שתנועת הגלגל {היא} בין הצפון (והימין) [והדרום] - ישרה תשובתו **מעולם לא ראינו וכו'.**

ורב אחא הביא ספק על תשובה זו, ואמר כי **דלמא כי סדנא דריחיא וכי צנורא דדשא** - ר"ל ואולי הגלגל בכללו יתנועע - עוגת המזלות עומדת

and the celestial sphere moves within it – as a mill moves within the vessel which surrounds it, which remains stationary, as does the wood that stands in the centre. Hence, though the mill continuously rotates, the vessel surrounding it and the wood that stands in the centre remain stationary. Thus does the celestial sphere revolve while the network of constellations is stationary, keeping its place, and [as a result] [the constellations in] the left [north], right [south], east, and west remain in place. This is the explanation of "like the steel [socket] of a mill."

The explanation of "like the pivot of a door" is, when the door rotates, it moves in whichever direction its pivot rotates; thus, the door's position changes while that of its pivot remains stationary.[1] [However] the truth is that this [second example] is highly unlikely, more unlikely than a fixed sphere and revolving constellations. [Nevertheless], there is no need for all of this since it has been clarified that the movement of the celestial sphere is between the corners of east and west, as we explained.

HaNasi's refutation due to an obvious flaw.

In an entirely opposite approach, the *Shiṭa Mequbeṣet* (*Ketubot* 13b) cites in the name of Rabbenu Tam:

> Rabbenu Tam said that although the wise men of the gentile nations defeated the Sages of Israel, the defeat was due only to their [sounder] claims; however, reality concurs with the Sages of Israel. That is why we say in our [Sabbth morning] prayer:
>
> [The God who opens daily the doors of the gates of the East] and splits open the windows of the firmament, [brings out the sun from its place, and the moon from the site of its abode].

See, however, R. David Ḥayim Shloush in *Ḥemda Genuza*, II (32):

> In our time, it is obvious and known to all that the wise men of the gentile nations are correct, and if the *Shiṭa Mequbeṣet* was alive in our time, he would retract his words…
>
> Regarding that which we say on the Sabbath day, "The God who opens daily the doors…" – it is purely poetic theory. Moreover, it seems that this passage was not part of the [original] enactment [of the liturgy] of the Men of the Great Assembly. [For] it is not written in the *siddur* of the R. Saạdiah Gaon nor in the *siddur* of HaRaMBa"M. It seems that it was added into the *siddur* by some sage to strengthen the opinion of the *Shiṭa Mequbeṣet*…

R' Yosef Ḥayim of Baghdad in *Rav Peạlim* (II, *Sod Yesharim* 3) explains the *siddur's* text in a mystical fashion in light of modern astronomy.

1 Meaning, *Ạgala* and *Ạqrav* are at the centre of the sphere's rotation and therefore remain in their respective positions.

במקומה, והגלגל סובב בתוך העוגה - **כאשר תנוד הרחיים בתוך הכלי הסובב אותה, שהוא עומד, ולא תנוד העץ האמצעי שעומד בתוך ג"כ. הנה שאע"פ שהרחיים סובבת וחוזרת ותשובנה הליכתה,** {בכל זאת} **הכלי הסובב אותה - והעץ העומד בתוכה - קיים ועומד במקומו. כן יהיה הגלגל סובב ועוגת המזלות עומד ישמור מקומו, ולא ינוד השמאלי והימיני המזרחי והמערבי - זהו פירוש כי סדנא דריחיא.**

ופירוש כי צנורא דדשא - ר"ל כאשר יסוב ינוד הדלת על מקומות שהציר סובב כאשר תסוב הדלת על צירה שעקר הדלת סובב ומשתנה מקומו, והציר עומד ולא ינוד. והאמת כי זה רחוק, ויותר רחוק מגלגל קבוע ומזלות חוזרים, ואין צורך לכל זה כיון שנתברר שתנועת הגלגל {היא} **בין פאתי מזרח ומערב כאשר ביארנו.**

It was stated at the end of this *beraita*: **the Sages of Israel say that during the day, the sun travels underneath the firmament, and at night above the firmament.** This opinion is undoubtedly dependent on [their earlier] view of a stationary celestial sphere and revolving constellations.[1] [The *beraita* continues:] **The wise men of the gentile nations say that during the day, the sun travels above the Earth, and at night underneath the Earth**. This opinion is undoubtedly dependent on [their earlier] view of a revolving sphere and stationary constellations.[2]

When Ribbi heard these words, which are undoubtedly dependent on [the earlier] dispute, he proved the opinion of the gentile scholars with his statement "their words appear more accurate, as we see that during the day, the springs are cold, while at night they are hot."[3] [Nevertheless] [Ribbi's] proof is extremely weak, as you can observe.[4]

And now, contemplate what has been taught us in this *beraita* and how precious is the matter that we have learned [from it]. For Ribbi only analysed these opinions through the process of proofs, without placing upon his heart [any bias or favour] towards the Sages of Israel towards nor to the wise men of the gentile nations. He only decided according to the wise men of the gentile nations due to the proof

1 Although it seemingly appears that this debate is separate a debate from the previous one, Rabbenu Avraham interprets it to be a consequential outcome of the former view. Perhaps this is because according to the opinion of the Sages of Israel that the stars do not actually rotate around the Earth [but rather shift away and reappear]; consequently the sun would do the same.

2 Here too, since the wise men of the gentile nations believed that the stars moved by virtue of the sphere's rotation, the sun, too, would naturally rotate, without any independent ability to maneuver beyond the firmament.

3 Accordingly, Ribbi Yehudah HaNasi retracted his previous refutation of their opinion.

4 This is likely referring to the fact that, by Rabbenu Avraham's time, it was already known that the Earth is round, and therefore that the sun would not come any closer at night (for in fact, it is actually distanced further). See R. Se'ạdya Gaon's commentary to *Sefer Yeṣira* (ed. R. Qafiḥ, p. 83) where he explains that although the accepted view in his time was that the Earth is round, some of the early Sages believed it to be flat. See also *Guide* I, 31.

ואמר בסוף הברייתא חכמי ישראל אומרים ביום חמה הולכת למטה מן הרקיע ובלילה למעלה מן הרקיע. ודעת זו בלי ספק דבוקה ל{שיטת} **גלגל קבוע ומזלות חוזרין. וחכמי אומות העולם אומרים ביום חמה מהלכת למעלה מן הארץ, ובלילה למטה מן הארץ. ודעת זו בלי ספק דבוקה ל**{שיטת} **גלגל חוזר ומזלות קבועין.**

וכאשר שמע רבי הדברים האלה - שהם תוצאות מן ההקדמות שחלקו בהם תחילה - הכריע דעת חכמי אומות העולם בראיה זו שאמר **נראים דבריהם שביום מעינות צוננין ובלילה מעינות רותחין.** והנה זה עם היות ראיה זו רפה וחלושה כאשר אתה רואה.

ועתה, התבונן מה שהורונו בברייתא זו, ומה יקר עניינה שלמדנו. כי רבי לא הביט בדעת אלו אלא מדרך הראיות, בלי להשים על לב {שום נטייה ומשוא פנים} **- לא לחכמי ישראל ולא לחכמי אומות העולם. והכריע דעת חכמי אומות העולם**

which he thought was valid, that **during the, day the springs are cold, while at night they are hot.**

Contemplate this intelligent principle, for Ribbi did not settle [conclusively] according to the wise men of the gentile nations; rather, he was inclined towards their opinion over the opinion [of the Sages of Israel] due to his analysis, based on his observations, as we have mentioned. That is the meaning of his statement "Their words appear [more accurate]," [which is] an expression of inclination [not decisive conclusion]. However, if it would have been made clear to him in an absolute manner, and with proof, that the sphere revolves and the constellations are stationary, he would have concluded definitively in accordance with their opinion, just as other Sages have done regarding other matters, stating, "the wise men of the gentile nations have defeated the Sages of Israel."[1]

---

1 HaRaMBa"M writes:

> You should not find it unusual that the opinion of Aristotle disagrees with that of the Sages, of blessed memory, regarding this point. For this view, meaning, the one according to which the heavenly bodies emit sounds, is consequent upon the conviction in a fixed sphere [*galgal qavuạ*] and revolving constellations [*mazalot ḥozerim*]. And you already know, that in these astronomical matters they preferred the opinion of the wise men of the gentile nations over their own. For they explicitly state: The wise men of the gentile nations were victorious. (*Guide* II, 8)

R. Reuben Margaliot (*Milḥamot Hashem*, p. 88, note 31) notes that Rabbenu Avraham's text is different from his father's. For from the *Guide* it is implied that the end of the text in *Pesaḥim* states "The wise men of the gentile nations were victorious." However, Rabbenu Avraham states that Ribbi was merely inclined towards the gentiles' opinion. Furthermore, he clearly states that they would say "the wise men of the gentile nations have defeated the Sages of Israel" regarding "other matters" (דעות אחרות), not the matters at hand.

The text that Rabbenu Avraham quotes concurs with that of the standard Vilna edition, whereas the text in the Guide is that which is found in *Shiṭa Mequbeṣet, Ketubot* 13b.

In *Torah, Chazal & Science*, Rabbi Meiselman uses this contradiction as the strongest support for his theory that this work was affected by interpolations:

> It would be very surprising if Rabbeinu Avraham knew of both variants of the Gemara yet chose to ignore the one cited by his father and base an argument specifically upon the alternative. Hence if one wishes to maintain that Rabbeinu Avraham is the author of this section, one must conjecture that he did not even know of his father's text, which would be very strange indeed. (p. 109)

R. Moshe Maimon (ibid., p.42) suggests that one should not place too great an emphasis on the Hebrew translation, and that the words "דעות אחרות" (which we translated as "other matters") may in fact mean "סברות אחרות" (other reasonings) or

מפני ראיה זו שחשב כי היא ראיה מתקבלת, שביום מעינות צוננין ובלילה מעינות רותחין.

והתבונן חכמת זה הסוד כי רבי לא פסק {בהחלט} כדעת חכמי אומות העולם, אלא שהכריע דעתם מדעת {חכמי ישראל על ידי} שיקול הדעת בראיה שזכרנו, {ו}זהו שאמר נראים דבריהם {ש}הוא מלה {=ביטוי} מורה על הכרעה {ולא פסק מוחלט}. ואילו נתברר לו בודאי ובראיה שגלגל חוזר ומזלות קבועים היה פוסק הלכה כמותם {בהחלט}, כאשר עשו זולתו מן החכמים ז"ל בדעות אחרות ואמרו נצחו חכמי אומות העולם לחכמי ישראל.

Truly, this master is to be called *Rabbenu HaQadosh* (Our Holy Rabbi), for when one removes falsehood and upholds the truth, when he is inclined towards the truth and retracts previous assumptions, there is no doubt that he is holy.[1]

"טיעונים אחרים" (other arguments) – meaning that other Sages [besides Ribbi] concurred with the wise men of the gentile nations regarding the celestial spheres due to other reasons or arguments. For it is possible that the standard text of the Talmud lacks a portion of the original dialogue, which may have contained further arguments and reasonings, and which concluded with "The wise men of the gentile nations were victorious." Accordingly, both HaRaMBa"M and Rabbenu Avraham saw the same text. Rather HaRaMBa"M focused on the anonymous opinion of the Sages, while Rabbenu Avraham focused on Ribbi's indecision. (See *She'elot uTeshuvot MaHaRa"M ElAshkar*, 96, which refers to responsa of R. Sherira and R. Hai Gaon in which other proofs that are absent from our standard text are mentioned.)

Alternatively, it can be posited that HaRaMBa"M (in the *Guide*) is not citing from the Talmud in *Pesaḥim*, but rather from some other statement of the Sages (see, for example, *Midrash Hagadol* to Genesis 1:17). Rabbenu Avraham was fully aware of this statement, and therefore cites it in relation to the topic at hand since the subject matter is nearly identical.

R. Meiselman (ibid.) writes: "it would be very surprising if Rabbenu Avraham knew of both variants of the Gemara yet chose to ignore the one cited by his father." However, we do see that Rabbenu Avraham in *HaMaspiq* (*Hilkhot Berakhot*; ed. R. Pinḥas Qoraḥ, p. 65) disputes his father's ruling due to a textual discrepancy in the Talmud. For HaRaMBa"M rules that the morning blessings "…Who did not create me a gentile/ slave/ woman" may be recited whether one has seen them or not. However, Rabbenu Avraham mentions that he saw an earlier edition of the Talmud with R. Isaac Alfasi's commentary which reads "when one sees a gentile one recites… and so too concerning a woman and a slave," implying that one must indeed see them if they are to recite the blessing.

This differs from R. Meiselman's statement (p. 87 [footnote]) that R. Yaakov Wincelberg was aware of only one instance where Rabbenu Avraham disputes with his father; namely, concerning the washing of the hands on Yom Kippur. See also Rabbenu Avraham's commentary to the Torah (Genesis 24:12), where he seemingly disputes his father's approach to the omen of Eliẹzer, servant of Avraham (*Hilkhot Ạvoda Zara* 11:4). Furthermore, R. Moshe Maimon (*Perush HaTorah LeRabbenu Avraham ben HaRaMB"aM* [Exodus, p. 18, footnote 40] lists five places where Rabbenu Avraham disputes his father in exposition of the text.

1 The Talmud (*Shabbat* 118b) gives an alternative reason for this title: "'Why did they call you our Holy Rabbi?' He (R. Yehudah HaNasi) said to them, 'It is because in all my days I never looked at my circumcision'…he did not insert his hand below his belt."

Although Ribbi himself answered the question, it is difficult to grasp that such a private matter of piety would cause him to be known to all as "our Holy Rabbi." It is possible that Ribbi was responding humbly, for he did not want to speak of his

ובאמת נקרא אדון זה רבינו הקדוש, כי האדם כשישליך מעל פניו השקר ויקיים האמת ויכריענו לאמיתו ויחזור בו מדעתו כשיתבאר לו הפכה, אין ספק כי קדוש הוא.

Behold, it has been clarified to us that the Sages, of blessed memory, exclusively assessed opinions based on truth and evidence, not based on who said them, as [a correct opinion should be accepted] regardless of who said it.[1]

Upon [completing] this preface [I will now proceed] to say - and from God I ask assistance that I may observe the truth: that all of the various *derashot*[2] found in the works of [the Sages] – in the Talmud or in any other work – fall into five categories [and the narratives which we have mentioned fall into four categories].

◆◆◆

own greatness in Torah, *middot*, or *deọt*. Similarly, in his introduction to *Commentary to the Mishna*, HaRaMBa"M attaches other qualities to Ribbi Yehudah HaNasi, in addition to the name he was given:

> ...Rabbenu HaQadosh, peace be upon him, was unique in his generation – a man that God graced with good character traits and piety, to the point that he merited to be called our Holy Rabbi by the people of his generation. His name is Judah. He was complete in wisdom and virtue, as they stated (*Giṭin* 59a), "From the days of Moses, our teacher, and until Ribbi, we did not see Torah and grandeur in one place." He was complete in piety and humility and in distancing himself from physical desires. (ed. R. Qafiḥ, p.8)

1 It is of note that Rabbenu Avraham did not use Ribbi's conversations with Antoninus (see *Sanhedrin* 91b) as an example of this, for Ribbi himself humbly admitted to Antoninus' opinions regarding esoteric concepts such as the time of the placement of a soul in a body, or the point that the evil inclination comes to power. Perhaps Rabbenu Avraham specifically selected a case where Ribbi changed his mind in the face of the opposing opinion of the Sages of Israel.

2 homiletical exegeses tied to specific passages of Scripture

והנה נתברר לנו כי החכמים ז"ל אינם מעיינים הדעות ולא מביטין אותם, אלא מצד אמיתתם ומצד ראיותיהם, לא מפני האומר אותו - יהיה מי שיהיה.

ואחר ההקדמה הזאת אומר - ומה' אשאל עזר על התבוננות האמת - כי כל הדרשות הנמצאות בדבריהם ז"ל, בתלמוד ובשאר מקומות, מתחלקות לחמשה חלקים, [והמעשיות שהזכירו מתחלקות לארבעה חלקים].

◆◆◆

Chapter 3

The five categories of exegesis

3:1 – Simple Exegeses

The first of the five categories of exegeses are those exegetical passages which are to be interpreted according to their simple meaning. Nothing other than the simple meaning and that which is apparent to the reader was intended in them. Although this category is easily understood and does not require an example, I will [nevertheless] provide one for additional clarification. The matter mentioned in *Berakhot*[1] is illustrative of this:

> **Ribbi Yoḥanan said in the name of Ribbi Shimon ben Yoḥai, "One is forbidden to fill his mouth with laughter in this world, as the verse states,** *then will our mouths fill with laughter and our lips with song; then will they say among the nations, the Lord has done great things with these.*[2] **When** will our mouths fill with laughter and our lips with song? When *they will say amongst the nations, the Lord has done great things with these.*"[3]

3:2 – Exegeses in which the Simple Meaning Conflicts with the True Meaning

The second category are those exegetical passages which contain both a literal and a hidden [meaning]. The focus [of this type of exegesis] was [actually] on the hidden meaning, not the literal meaning. However, for several reasons they [the Sages] formed it in a literal manner such that the literal meaning stands in opposition to the hidden meaning. Most of these [reasons], though not all, have already

1 31a

2 Psalms 126:2

3 Although the simple explanation of the verse would not be understood as such, nevertheless the moral teaching extracted from its homiletical interpretation (*derasha*) should be understood at face value.

פרק ג

חמשה חלקי הדרשות

ג:א - דרשות כפשוטן

החלק הראשון מחלקי הדרשות החמשה הם דרשות על פי פשוטן - לא נתכוון בהם דבר אחר זולת הפשט והנראה בעיני ההוגים. והחלק הזה עם היותו מבואר ואינו צריך דמיון {=דוגמא}, אודיעך דמיונו לתוספות ביאור.

והוא כענין מה שאמרו במסכת ברכות[יט] **א"ר יוחנן משום ר' שמעון בן יוחאי אסור לאדם שימלא שחוק פיו בעולם הזה שנאמר אז ימלא שחוק פינו [ולשוננו רנה, אז יאמרו בגוים הגדיל ה' לעשות עם אלה. אימתי ימלא שחוק פינו ולשוננו רנה, בזמן שיאמרו בגוים הגדיל ה' לעשות עם אלה].**

ג:ב - דרשות שפשוטן מנוגד לטעמן האמיתי

החלק השני [מהן] - הדרשות שיש [להן] נגלה ונסתר, והכוונה היתה הענין הנסתר ולא הענין הנגלה [ממנה]. ו[אמנם] שמו לה ענין נגלה היפך ענינו הנסתר לכמה תועליות, כבר נתבארו רובם,

been explained in the *Guide for the Perplexed*[1] and the *Commentary to the Mishna.*[2] An example of this category is the statement in *Taạnit*:[3]

> **Ribbi Ḥelbo said** that **Ụlla [of] Bira'a said** that **Ribbi Elạzar said, "The Holy One, blessed is He, is destined to arrange a dance for the righteous in the Garden of Eden, and He shall stand among them, and each and every one** of the righteous **will point at Him with his finger, as the verse states,** *And it shall be said on that day: Behold, this is our God; we have waited for Him, and He delivered us. This is the Lord, for whom we waited. We will be glad and rejoice in His salvation.*"[4]

Behold, the literal meaning of this exegesis will distance anyone possessing intellect and faith from believing it.[5] [However], there is no doubt that the [actual] hidden meaning intended by its author [Ribbi Elạzar] should be believed by one who possesses faith and intellect, for it is true.

And it [the hidden meaning of the above passage] is that the reward of the righteous in the World to Come will be [their ability] to comprehend [directly] from Him, Exalted be He, that which is impossible to attain in this world. This is the [main] purpose of reward [in the World to Come] and the height of delight.[6]

He [Ribbi Elạzar] allegorised this [initial state of] happiness as a dance,[7] and the ability of each individual to comprehend Him, Praised

1 See, for example, *Guide* I, 46 and *Guide* II, 6.

2 See, for example, the introduction to *Pereq Ḥeleq*.

3 31a

4 Psalms 126:2

5 Elsewhere (*Milḥamot HaShem*) Rabbenu Avraham explains:

> Every properly believing and intelligent person knows that it is impossible that it should be understood literally, because the Holy One, blessed be He, is not a body that stands, towards which one might point a finger.

6 As HaRaMBa"M writes (*Hilkhot Teshuva* 8:2):

> What is meant by the expression, "they will delight in the radiance of the Divine Presence"? That they will comprehend the truth of Godliness which they cannot grasp while in a dark and humble body.

7 Traditional dancing represents a collective state of happiness in which all participants move together.

אבל לא כולם, במורה ובפירוש המשנה. ודמיון החלק הזה {הוא} **אמרם בגמרא תעניות[י] [אמר ר' חלבו אמר עולא ביראה] אמר ר' אלעזר עתיד הקב"ה לעשות מחול לצדיקים בגן עדן והוא עומד ביניהן, וכל אחד ואחד מראה לו באצבעו, שנאמר ואמר ביום ההוא הנה אלהינו זה [קוינו לו ויושיענו זה ה' קוינו לו נגילה ונשמחה בישועתו].**

הנה {פשט ה}נגלה {ב}דרש הזה ירחיק כל בעל שכל וכל בעל אמונה מלהאמינו. והענין הנסתר שנתכוין עליו אומרו, [אין ספק שהכוונה בו] יש לבעל אמונה ושכל להאמין אותו [מפני] שהוא האמת. והיינו, ששכרן של צדיקים הנזכרים לחיי עולם הבא הוא השגתם ממנו יתעלה מה שאי אפשר להשיג בעולם הזה, וזוהי תכלית הזכייה ושיא האושר.

והמשיל אותה השמחה במחול. והמשיל מה שהגיע כל אחד מהם בהשגתו יתעלה באמרו וכל א' וא'

be He, by his statement "each and every one will point at Him with his finger."[1] He [then] demonstrates that this state of comprehension is the ultimate yearning by his statement "Behold, this is our God, for whom we waited…" He [then] demonstrates the reward and the evasion of true doom in the World to Come, by his statement "and He delivered us." He [then] demonstrates the true happiness and delight which shall then be attained by his statement "We will be glad and rejoice in His salvation."

This is the purpose of brevity of speech and the beauty of allegory and symbol in [imparting] many spiritual matters in few words. Based upon this [analysis], one may compare all similar [exegeses].

3:3 – Exegeses which Present Difficulty in Understanding their Simple Meanings

The third category are exegeses which do not contain a hidden meaning, as their author only intends [to convey] their revealed meaning, yet comprehending this revealed meaning is difficult to the point that it will not be grasped by most who analyse them. And [even] if it would be comprehended, the comprehension would be deficient or distorted. The majority of exegeses in this category will often be misconstrued due to the difficulties of the subject and terminology. [Meaning,] the reader will not understand which concept was intended from the words employed by the author, nor if the words were meant to portray multiple concepts.

And this category, in relation to difficulty and ambiguity, is similar to the previous[2] category, except that at times it is [even] more difficult [to understand the meaning of such an exegesis]. Thus, one must

1 Elsewhere (*Milḥamot HaShem*) Rabbenu Avraham explains:

> "Each and every one will point at Him with his finger" is a metaphor for the specific knowledge which separates His holiness from the holiness of His angels. This is the secret meaning of the partition which separates Him from His creations. The wise will understand.

2 The new scholarly translation of the Arabic fragments reads "לחלק הראשון" – "to the first category" – which is difficult to understand since the first category delineated above concerns those exegeses which are to be understood simply. The translation here follows the Oxford edition, which reads "לחלק שלפניו" – "to the previous section."

מראה לו באצבעו. והוכיח על היות ההשגה הזאת שיא התקוה ותכלית התוחלת באמרו **הנה אלהינו זה** {קוינו לו וגו'}. והוכיח על הזכייה וההמלטות מן האובדן האמיתי בעולם הבא באמרו **ויושיענו.** והוכיח על השמחה והאושר האמיתי שישיגו אז באמרו **נגילה ונשמחה בישועתו.**

וזהו תכלית בקצרות הדיבור ויפי המשלת המשל והרמיזה לעניינים רבים רוחניים במילים מועטות. ולפי זה תקיש על {כל} הדומה לזה.

ג:ג - דרשות שקשה להבין הפשט הפשוט שלהן

החלק השלישי [מהן] - דרשות שאין להם ענין נסתר אלא כוונת האומרן הוא נגליהן בלבד, אלא שהבנת הנגלה ההוא יקשה על רוב המעיינים עד שלא יובן, ואם יובן, תהיה הבנה חסירה או משובשת. ולפעמים יראה מרוב דרשות החלק הזה הפוך כוונתן לקושי הענינים ולהשתתפות המלות, ו{היינו ש}לא ידע הרואה איזה ענין נתכוון האומר מעניני המלות ההם אשר יורו עליו, או שלא יבין אם המלות ההם נאמרו בשיתוף על שני ענינים או יותר.

וזה החלק מבחינת הקושי וההעלמה קרוב לחלק הראשון, אלא שבמקצת מקומות הוא יותר קשה מן הראשון. ו{לכן} צריך להזהר בו, ולא יפליג

be cautious in it and must not augment its explanations in order to prevent mistakes and misinterpretations. An example of this category can be found in *Berakhot*:[1]

> **One must always incite *(yargiz)* his good inclination *(yeṣer ṭov)* against his evil inclination *(yeṣer harạ)*, as the verse states, *tremble, and sin no more.*[2] If he overcame it, it is good, but if not, he should occupy himself with Torah, for the verse states, *say in your heart.*[3] If he overcame it, it is good, but if not, he should recite *Qeriat Shemạ*, as the verse states, *upon your bed.*[4] If he overcame it, it is good, but if not, he should remember the day of death, as the verse states, *and be forever still.*[5]**

This exegesis has no other purpose besides its revealed meaning. However, it is difficult to comprehend this revealed meaning due to a lack in definition of the terms "good" and "evil" inclinations.[6] He [the reader] will also find it difficult to understand the reasons for all [the remedies] mentioned in this matter. [Therefore], I shall explain it, in order that you understand it and relate it to all similar [exegeses of this nature].

The connotation of *yargiz* is to rule and triumph, and *yeṣer hatov* refers to the intellect, and *yeṣer harạ* – in this context – [refers to] physical desires and other similar [human] shortcomings.

The intended meaning of the passage "One should always *yargiz*" is that a man's intellect must always rule his over his desires, by means of coherent and properly aligned thought.[7] If this is enough to subdue

1 5a

2 Psalms 4:5

3 Ibid.

4 Ibid.

5 Ibid.

6 Although there is an awareness that the good and evil inclinations exist, the philosophical mechanics of these concepts require further elucidation.

7 We are enlightened as to the nature of these thoughts by the words of HaRaMBa"M:

> They [the Sages] stated that one should turn himself and his thought to matters of Torah, and expand his knowledge of wisdom, for immoral sexual thoughts only become

בפירושו כדי שלא תפול טעות ויציאה מן המכוון.

ודוגמת חלק זה מה שאמרו בגמרא בברכות[יא] **לעולם ירגיז אדם יצר טוב על יצר הרע שנאמר רגזו ואל תחטאו,** [אם נצחו מוטב ואם לאו יעסוק בתורה שנאמר אמרו בלבבכם], **אם נצחו מוטב, ואם לאו יקרא קרית שמע שנאמר על משכבכם, אם נצחו מוטב ואם לאו יזכור יום המיתה שנאמר ודומו סלה.**

ואין כוונת דרשה זו זולתי נגלתה, אלא שהבנת נגלתה יקשה מחמת העלם הוראת יצר טוב ויצר הרע כאן. וגם יקשה להבין הטעם לכל מה {ש} הוזכר בענין. ואני אעירך על זה כדי שתבינהו ותקיש גם על כל כיוצא בזה, ואומר שכוונת ירגיז היא השליטה והנצחון, ויצר טוב הוא השכל, ויצר הרע כאן {הוא} התאוות הגופניות וכיוצא בהן מן החסרונות.

וכוונת מאמרו {לעולם ירגיז וכו' היינו} שיהא האדם תמיד משליט שכלו על תאוותיו על ידי מחשבה ישרה ומכוונת. ואם מספיק זה להכנעת

his desires – that is to say, if proper thought and contemplation suffice – it is good. But if not, he shall strengthen his thought by engaging in recitation of Scripture [as speech is the vessel of intellect, and by the combination of proper speech with contemplation of what he is reciting], he shall strengthen his thought and curb it from wandering and neglect.[1] If this is enough, it is good, and if not, he should recite *Qeriat Shemą* and contemplate upon its meaning.

Qeriat Shemą was specified for two reasons, the first – and weaker – reason is because there is a correlation between what the verse [cited in the passage] states – *upon your bed*, and what the verse of *Qeriat Shemą* states – *when you lie down*.[2] This is a syntactical *gezera shava* (a clarification based on identical terms), of the form of halakhic comparisons.

The second [reason] – the stronger of the two – is because *Qeriat Shemą* contains exalted matters which are the objectives of the good inclination; namely, the Oneness [of God], love and servitude towards Him, and [the awareness of] reward and punishment. Within it there exists [the concept of] great submission of the evil inclination, for He, the Exalted One, said, *and you shall not wander after your hearts and after your eyes*,[3] and tremendous encouragement of the good inclination, for it says, *and you shall be holy*[4] *to your God, I am the Lord your God...*[5]

The passage then states that if the evil inclination is rash and triumphant, to the point where even this [third] tier will be insufficient to subdue it, he

strengthened in a heart devoid of wisdom. (*Hilkhot Isurei Bi'ah* 22:21)

1 Thus, the second tier of advice is built upon the first, for it utilises the element of speech to increase the effectiveness of thought.

2 Deuteronomy 6:7. The Hebrew "על משכבכם" (*upon your bed*) and "ובשכבך," (*when you lie down*) share the same root, ש-כ-ב.

3 Numbers 15:39

4 Being holy requires the subordination of the *yeṣer harą*. Thus, this constitutes a "tremendous encouragement" endorsed by the *Qeriat Shemą*.

5 Ibid. Thus, the third tier of advice is also built on that which precedes it, for it provides a specific type of thought to contemplate (that is to say, the first tier) while reciting verses (the second tier).

תאוותיו - כלומר {שיספיק} המחשבה והתבוננות הנכונה - מוטב, ואם לא יחזק מחשבתו על ידי עסק הזכרת פסוקים, [מפני שהדיבור כלי השכל, ועל ידי השימוש בדיבור הראוי יחד עם המחשבה בכוונת מה שאומר] יחזק המחשבה ויגבילהו מהשוטטות וההזנחה. [ואם זה מספיק {מוטב}, ואם לאו] יקרא קרית שמע ויתבונן בכוונתה.

וייחד קרית שמע לשתי סיבות, האחת מהן - והיא החלשה שבהן - [ההוכחה מפסוק המקביל לזה] לפי שיש הוכחה מזה שאמר[כב] {הכתוב} **על משכבכם**, וקרית שמע נאמר בה[כג] **ובשכבך**, וזו גזירה שוה בלשון על דרך היקשיהם ההלכתיים.

והשניה - והיא החזקה שבהן - מפני שבקרית שמע יש הזכרה בדברים מרוממים שהם תכלית יצר הטוב - והם הייחוד והאהבה והעבודה, והשכר והעונש - ובה הכנעה יתירה של יצר הרע מפני שאמר יתעלה בה[כד] **ולא תתורו אחרי לבבכם ואחרי עיניכם**, וחיזוק עצום של יצר הטוב מפני שאמר בה[כה] **והייתם קדושים לאלהיכם אני ה' אלהיכם וכו'**.

ואז אמר שאם יש ביצר הרע קלות ראש ומידת הניצוח, באופן שלא יספיק להכניעו ואף לא בדרגא

shall subdue it by the contemplation of death and cessation. By this shall the evil inclination be broken, as Ạqavia b. Mahalalel said: "Reflect upon three things, and you will not come to the hands of transgression: Know from where you came, where you are going, and before Whom you are destined to give a judgment and account."[1] One may draw an analogy from this [example] to other similar [exegeses of this category].

3:4 – Exegeses Stated Succinctly by the Sages in the Manner of Poetry

The fourth category refers to exegeses in which the Sages, peace be upon them, explained verses in a poetic or rhetorical style. The one relating it does not actually believe that the exegesis represents the actual intention of the given verse. Regarding this and cases similar to it, the Sages, of blessed memory, said "Scripture and *Midrash* are distinct one from the other."[2] An example of this category is the passage in *Taạnit*:[3]

> **Ribbi Yoḥanan said, "What is the meaning of that which is written,** *A tithe* **(ạsser)** *shall you tithe* **(te'ạsser)**[4]**? Tithe (*ạsser*) in order that you become wealthy (*te'ạsher*)."**[5]

Another example [of this category] is the [following] passage,[6] which explains that which He, may He be Exalted, said:

1 *Avot* 3:5

2 This phrase is not found in the standard Talmud. R. Margaliot directly sources it to the phrase found in *Avoda Zara* 58b and *Ḥulin* 137b: "לשון תורה לעצמה לשון חכמים לעצמן" [The language of the Torah and the language of the Sages are distinct one from the other]. This is difficult to understand, since the context of the phrase is used only to show that the Sages used Hebrew words in a manner different from the Torah, whereas Rabbenu Avraham is portraying the dichotomy between the actual intent of the verse and the Rabbinic interpretation. R. Moshe Maimon (ibid., p.53) notes that Tanḥum haYerushalmi, a contemporary of Rabbenu Avraham, uses the same phrase.

3 9a

4 Deuteronomy 14:22

5 This exegesis is poetic by virtue of the *sin* replacement with a *shin*. Nevertheless, we do find instances of letter-replacement which carry halakhic ramifications (e.g. הילול to חילול [*Berakhot* 35a]).

6 Ibid.

הזו, אז יכניעהו בזכרון המות והסוף. ובזה תהיה תכלית שבירת יצר הרע, כמו שאמר עקביה בן מהללאל[כו] **הסתכל בג' דברים [ואין אתה בא לידי עבירה, דע מאין באתה ולאין אתה הולך ולפני מי אתה עתיד ליתן דין וחשבון.** ומכאן הקש על כל כיוצא בזה].

ג:ד - דרשות שנאמרו מדעת החכמים ז"ל דרך צחות כמליצת השיר

החלק הרביעי [מהן] - דרשות שאמרו ע"ה אותו בביאור פסוקים בדרך מליצת השיר, לא מפני שהאומרה סובר שכוונת זה הפסוק היא זאת הדרשה. ועל כיוצא בזה אמרו ז"ל מקרא לחוד ומדרש לחוד.

ודוגמא לחלק הזה אומרם בגמרא תעניות[כז] **אמר ר' יוחנן מאי דכתיב עשר תעשר, עשר בשביל שתתעשר.** ו{חלק זה הוא גם} **דוגמת אמרם שם**[כח]

...and I shall pour out for you a blessing such that there shall be more than sufficiency.[1] **What is** the meaning of the phrase *such that there shall be more than sufficiency* (עַד בְּלִי דָי)? **That your lips will be worn out** (יִבְלוּ) **from saying 'enough'** (דַי).[2]

By this method should one approach similar types [of exegesis]. Do not think that every verse-explanatory statement of the Sages, of blessed memory, was given into their hands by tradition, as the masses – who have not arrived at an accurate knowledge – think. For they say that just as the principles of *halakha* and [certain] teachings were passed through tradition, so too were all their words passed through tradition. Rather, know that explanations of verses which do not pertain to *halakha* or *dinim* are based [either] on [their own] comparison or assessment, or by means of poetic speech;[3] they layer what is possible to layer upon it [the verse] by way of clarification, in a poetic form.[4]

1 Malachi 3:10

2 This is poetic, as the word בְּלִי cannot actually mean בְּלִיָּה.

3 Rabbenu Avraham seemingly limits the Oral Law to explanations of verses that only pertain to *halakhot* or *dinim*. See, however, his use of the phrase in his comments to Genesis 46:26 and Exodus 2:1: "If it be a tradition, we accept it, but if it be an inference [based on one's own reasoning], there is [that is to say: can be] a refutation," which implies that there could, in some instances, exist traditions for non-halakhic teachings.

See also *Bava Batra* 91a in which the Talmud states the names of the mothers of Avraham, David, Shimshon and Haman (which are not stated in Scripture) in order to refute the heretics concerning the claim that there exists no tradition for their names (see RaSHBa"M's comments there).

Perhaps Rabbenu Avraham uses the phrase ["If it be a tradition..."] hyperbolically/rhetorically, and in reality, there cannot be a tradition for statements of this nature. Alternatively, perhaps here Rabbenu Avraham is solely negating the notion that all statements were given by tradition, though some may very well have been.

4 HaRaMBa"M writes similarly:

> As to the value of these Midrashic interpretations, there are two different schools of thought. The first school believes that a *midrash* contains the real explanation of the text, while the other, finding that it cannot be reconciled with the words quoted, rejects and ridicules it. The members of the first school of thought fight and exert themselves in order to prove and to confirm such interpretations according to their opinion, and to keep them as the real meaning of the text; they consider them in the same light as traditional laws. Neither of the two classes understood it [as it correctly should be], for [in reality] our Sages employ Biblical texts merely as poetical expressions, the meaning of which is clear to every

בביאור אומרו[יט] {יתעלה} **והריקותי לכם ברכה עד בלי די - מאי עד בלי די, עד שיבלו שפתותיכם מלומר די. ובדרך זה תקיש אל הדומה לו.**

ואל תחשוב שכל מאמר שיאמרוהו ז"ל בביאור הפסוקים הוא קבלה בידם, כמו שחושבים המון העם שלא הגיעו לידיעה מדויקת {ואומרים} שכמו שיסודות ההלכה והשמועות קבלה, כך כל דבריהם ז"ל קבלה. {שאין הדבר כן,} אלא דע שפירושים לפסוקים שאינם שייכים להלכה ולדינים, יש מהם {שהם} על דרך ההקשה וההכרעה, ויש בדרך של לשון צחות המליצה והיפוי, ומשיאים על המאמר מה שאפשר להשיא עליו על דרך הכשרת ההבנה כמליצות הפיוטיות.

[Know that] I have no doubt concerning the teaching of R. Joshua[1] in explaining [the phrase] "and Jethro heard":[2] "What hearing did he hear, and came? He heard of the war of Ạmaleq, and came." For this is based upon [his personal] comparison and assessment, as he did not receive this by way of tradition. A proof for this is due to the support he provides by stating, "For it is written adjacent to..."[3] [and if he had a tradition, he would not have had to bring a proof for his explanation].[4] Another proof [for this is seen in virtue of the] other Sages, of blessed memory, differing from him. [For] if it was a passed tradition, it cannot be subject to debate.[5] For R. Elạzar HaModạ'i states "he heard of the giving of the Torah and came," and he, too, provided support [for his teaching]. Furthermore, R. Eliezer states "he heard of the splitting of the Sea of Reeds and came," and he, too, provided support [for his teaching].

[Similarly] there exists no doubt that the explanation[6] "Speak (דַּבֵּר) to the Children of Israel, and let them journey ahead (וְיִסָּעוּ)"[7] – "He [Moses] lifted (הסיע) matters (דבר) from their heart" is merely constructed in a poetic form, and is not the [objective] explanation.[8]

reasonable reader. This style was general in ancient days; all adopted it in the same way as poets. (*Guide* III, 43)

1 *Zevaḥim* 116a

2 Exodus 18:1

3 adjacent to the verses concerning the war of Ạmaleq

4 The bracketed words appear in the Oxford editions.

5 Similarly, HaRaMBa"M writes:

> There has never been disagreement [among the sages] with regard to laws handed down by tradition. Anything concerning them, about which there has been disagreement, is certainly not a tradition dating back to Moses, our teacher. (*Hilkhot Mamrim* 1:3)
>
> Even the Sages themselves did not have a tradition regarding these matters and could only attempt to understand the verses. Thus, there were disagreements in these matters. (*Hilkhot Melakhim* 12:2)

6 *Mekhilta, Beshalaḥ* 3

7 Exodus 14:15

8 as the simple explanation of the word וְיִסָּעוּ means "they journeyed"

{ודע} **כי אני** לא אסתפק במאמר דברי ר' יהושע[ל] בפירוש וישמע יתרו[לא] - **מה שמועה שמע ובא, מלחמת עמלק שמע ובא, כי** {אמר} **זה** על ידי הקשה והכרעה, ולא שקבל {כן ב}קבלה. **וראייה** לזה היותו מנמק פירושו ואמר[לב] **שכן היא כתובה בצדה.** ו{עוד} **ראייה אחרת** - סברות זולתו מן החכמים ז"ל {הסוברים} **זולת הסברא הזאת, ואם היתה** {הדבר} קבלה מסורה **אין מחלוקת** {שייכת} בו. {והיינו} לפי שר' אלעזר המודעי אמר[לג] **מתן תורה שמע ובא**, ונימק {דבריו בראייה} **גם הוא**, ור' אליעזר אומר קריעת ים סוף **שמע ובא**, ו{הוא} נימק דבריו גם כן.

ו{כן} אין ספק שדברי האומר[לד] בביאור[לה] {הכתוב} **דבר אל בני ישראל ויסעו - הסיע דבר מליבן**, שזה על דרך צחות המליצה, לא על דרך ביאור.

[At times] the Sages, of blessed memory, bring exegeses of this category with no bearing on the [objective] explanation of the verse, but rather to stand independently, as, for example, the passage in *Rosh Hashana*[1] illustrates:

> *And the Canaanite, king of Arad, heard...*[2] **It was taught: Canaan, Siḥon, and Arad are identical.** He was named **Siḥon because he was similar to a foal (*siyaḥ*) in the desert,** and **Canaan on account of his kingdom, but what was his** true **name? Arad was his name.**[3]

It can be posited that the majority of exegeses found in the words of the Sages, of blessed memory, fall under this category, for they are beyond countable. And what we must agree upon - for it is the truth, and only the stubborn one will dispute this - is that this category of their [the Sages'] words contains many different variations, just as the different meanings of poems vary according to the knowledge of their authors. So too, every detail [*derasha*] in each category will differ according to the differences in wisdom and knowledge of each author.[4] [You must] contemplate this.

1 3a

2 Numbers 21:1

3 Exegeses of this style are allegorical and do not represent the actual historical identities of individuals. This style of identifying various entities as one is common throughout the works of the Sages. For example: "**Beọr** (father of Balaam), **Cushan-Rishạtayim, and Lavan the Aramean are identical.**" (*Sanhedrin* 105a).

Similarly to Rabbenu Avraham, Rabbi Avraham Ibn Ezra comments on Genesis 36:32:

> Belạ is not to be identified with Balaam, son of Beọr and neither is Balaam the son of Lavan the Aramean. The *midrash* which states that Balaam is the son of Lavan may be due to the fact that both were sorcerers.

This is contrary to the approach of Lurianic *Qabbala* (see *Shaạr haGilgulim* [Gates of Reincarnation]) which connects various personalities through reincarnation. For further reading on the rejection of reincarnation, see Se'ạdya Gaon, *Emunot veDeọt* (6, 8).

4 Accordingly, one should not be surprised by the constant contradictions between various exegeses, as each one manifests its author's own wisdom and knowledge.

ו{לפעמים} מביאים החכמים ז"ל דרשות מזה החלק בלי היותן ביאור פסוק, אלא עומדות בפני עצמן, כגון אומרם בגמרא ראש השנה[ג] {וישמע הכנעני מלך ערד וכו'} תנא הוא כנען הוא סיחון הוא ערד. סיחון שדומה לסיח במדבר, כנען על שם מלכותו, ומה שמו ערד שמו.

וכמעט יהיו רוב הדרשות הנמצאות בדבריהם ז"ל הם מזה החלק [, כי הם רבים מלספור]. וממה שצריכים להסכים בה - לפי שהוא האמת שלא יחלוק עליה אלא העקשן - הוא שהחלק הזה של דבריהם משתנה לשינויים רבים, כשינויי כוונת הפיוטים לפי שינויי הבנת אומריהם. וכך כל החלקים משתנים פרטיהם כפי שינויי חכמת אומריהם וידיעתם, והבן זה.

3:5 – Exegeses Stated by way of Hyperbole and Exaggeration

The fifth category relates to exegeses which contain exaggeration. An example of this category can be found found in *Pesaḥim*:[1] **"For Mar Zuṭra said, from Aṣel to Aṣal,**[2] [the Book of the Genealogies] **bore four hundred camel-loads of expositions."** [Its explanation is that] the first Aṣel is at the beginning of the verse, and the second is [at] its end: *To Aṣel, six sons, and these are their names: Azriqam, Bokhru, Ishmael, Sheạryah, Ọbadiah, and Ḥanan. All these are the sons of Aṣal.* Some commentators – in order to embellish this teaching – state that the first Aṣel is at the beginning of this verse, while the second is at the end of the following chapter: *To Aṣel, six sons…*[3] [This opinion would understand], however, that [the above] exegesis would refer to that which is between these two verses.

[In spite of this dispute,] according to both opinions, the passage is not free of great exaggeration; for no intelligent person can imagine that it would be possible to expound four hundred camel-loads of expositions [even] on the entirety of Scripture, surely much less on this smaller amount [of Scriptural content]. Indeed, this is an exaggeration, and others have already noted that this passage is an exaggeration.

This [fifth] category is small in comparison to the other [four] categories, for most of their [the Sages'] employment of this technique exists solely in narratives [*aggadot*], as we shall explain.

◆◆◆

1 62b

2 I Chronicles 8:38

3 Ibid 9:44

ג:ה - דרשות שנאמרו בגוזמא והפרזה

והחלק החמישי [מהן] - דרשות שיש בהן גוזמא. ודוגמת החלק הזה בגמרא פסחים[לז] **דאמר מר זוטרא מאצל לאצל הוי טעין ארבע מאה גמלי דרשא.** {וביאורו הוא ש}**אצל הראשון** {הוא} **תחילת פסוק**[לח] **ואצל האחרון** הוא סופו - **ולאצל ששה בנים ואלה שמותם עזריקם בכרו וישמעאל ושעריה ועבדיה וחנן כל אלה בני אצל.** ונאמר בדברי קצת מפרשים - כדי ליפות מאמר זה - כי **אצל** הראשון הוא התחלת פסוק זה, והאחרון הוא בסוף (הפסוק) [הפרשה] שאחרי זה[לט] - **ולאצל ששה בנים וכו'**, והדרש אמנם הוא על [מה שבין] שני פסוקים אלו.

ולפי שני הפירושים לא ימלט המאמר מגוזמא גדולה, כי לא ידמה משכיל שיתכן לדרוש על כל המקרא כולו משא ארבע מאות גמלים - וכל שכן על שיעור {מועט} זה ממנו. אמנם הוא גוזמא, וכבר העיר על זה זולתינו - כלומר {העירו} שמאמר זה הוא גוזמא.

והחלק הזה של הדרשות הוא מועט לעומת אלו החלקים האחרים, כי רוב השתמשותם של דרך זה - כלומר בגוזמא - אינו אלא במעשיות כמו שנבאר.

◆◆◆

Chapter 4

The four types of narratives

4:1 – Narratives which Occured in Reality

Regarding the four categories of narratives (*aggadot*): The first category is events that actually took place according to the manner in which they were related,[1] and were preserved due to the benefit that can be learned from them. This benefit may be legal, moral, or philosophical. Alternatively, they may be extraordinary [occurrences] in light of what preceded them [and were mentioned due to their remarkability]. This [first] category is divided into four types:[2]

4:1:1 – Narratives from which Legal Benefit may be Derived

The first type is narratives from which legal benefit may be derived – for example, the passage in the *Mishna* of *Sukka*:[3]

> **One whose head and majority** [of his body] **were in the *sukka*, and his table is in the house – the House of Shammai deem it** [this *sukka* arrangement] **invalid, and the House of Hillel deem it valid. The House of Hillel said to the House of Shammai, "Wasn't there an incident in which the Elders of the House of Shammai and the Elders of the House of Hillel went to visit Yoḥanan ben HaḤoroni, and they found him with his head and majority** [of his body] **in the *sukka*, and his table was in the house?!" the House of Shammai said to them, "From there** [do you seek to adduce] **a proof? For they** [the Elders of the House of Shammai] **too said to him, 'If you were accustomed to** [perform the *miṣva* in] **this** [manner], **you have never fulfilled the *miṣva* of *sukka* in all your days.'"**

1 Thus, the examples that will be cited are not to be taken metaphorically.

2 Namely, the four types which Rabbenu Avraham listed priorly: 1) legal, 2) moral, 3) philosophical, and 4) extraordinary.

3 *Sukka* 28a

פרק ד

ארבעה חלקי המעשיות

ד:א - מעשיות שאירעו במציאות

ו לגבי ארבעת חלקי המעשיות, הרי החלק הראשון [מהן] - מעשיות שקרו במציאות כפי מה שהזכירו, וקבעום עבור התועלת שיש לקבל ממנה. והתועלת ההיא תהיה בין בדינים או במדות או בדעות, או שיהיו אותן המעשיות {מאלו ש}רחוק שיארעו המתאימים למה שקדם להם [והוזכרו מפני נדירותם]. ויהיה החלק הזה מתחלק לארבעה מינים.

ד:א:א - מעשיות שאירעו שיש בהן תועלת בדינים

המין הראשון - הוא {המעשה} אשר יש ללמוד ממנו תועלת בדינים, כגון המאמר במשנת סוכה” **מי שהיה ראשו ורובו בסוכה [ושולחנו בתוך הבית בית שמאי פוסלין ובית הלל מכשירין] אמרו בית הלל לבית שמאי מעשה שהלכו זקני בית שמאי וזקני בית הלל לבקר את יוחנן בן החורוני ומצאוהו ראשו ורובו בסוכה ושלחנו בתוך הבית, אמרו להם בית שמאי משם ראייה, אף הם אמרו לו אם כן היית נוהג לא קיימת מצות סוכה מימיך.**

Another example [is found] in tractate *Ketubot*:[1]

> **The mother of Rami bar Ḥama wrote** a deed **in the morning** [transferring ownership] **of her property to Rami bar Ḥama, and in the evening she wrote** [another deed transferring her property] **to Rav Uqba bar Ḥama. Rami bar Ḥama came before Rav Sheshat and established his** [right to the] **property. Rav Uqba came before Rav Naḥman and established his** [right to the] **property. Rav Sheshat came before Rav Naḥman and said to him, "What is the reason that Master did this?" He (Rav Naḥman) said to him, "And what is the reason that Master did this?" He (Rav Sheshat) said to him, "For it** [Rami bar Ḥama's deed] **preceded** [that of Rav Uqba]. **He (Rav Naḥman) said to him, "Are we sitting in Jerusalem that we** [should] **write hours** [in legal documents]?"[2] [Rav Sheshat said to Rav Naḥman] **"Rather what is the reason that the Master did this?" He (Rav Naḥman) said to him (Rav Sheshat), "It was judges' discretion."** [Rav Sheshat said] **"I also** [applied] **judges' discretion." He (Rav Naḥman) said to him (Rav Sheshat), "Firstly** [in response to you I shall say that] **I am a judge, and the Master is not a judge. And furthermore, you did not initially arrive at it** (your conclusion) **due to this** [reason]."[3]

The specific instances of this type are innumerable.

4:1:2 Narratives which Contain Moral Virtue

The second type [in this category] is a narrative from which moral benefit may be derived, such as the passage in *Shabbat*:[4]

> **One must always be humble like Hillel, and not exacting like Shammai.** It once happened that **two individuals bet against each other, saying "Anyone who will go and aggravate Hillel will take four hundred *zuz* from his friend." One said, "I will go." That day**

1 94b

2 The Halakha states that in any place where the hours are not recorded on legal documents, there exists no precedence between documents written on the same day.

3 As mentioned, nearly every story that Rabbenu Avraham cites varies from the text of the standard Vilna edition.

4 30b–31a

ו{עוד דוגמא}, כגון דבריהם בגמרא כתובות[מב] אמיה דרמא בר חמא בצפרא כתבתינהו לנכסה לרמא בר חמא, באורתא כתבתינהו לרב עוקבא בר חמא, אתא רמי בר חמא לקמיה דרב ששת אוקמיה בנכסי, אתא רב עוקבא בר חמא לקמיא דרב נחמן אוקמיה בניכסי, אתא רב ששת לקמיה דרב נחמן אמר ליה [מאי טעמא עבד מר הכי, אמר ליה דקדים, אמר ליה אטו בירושלים יתבינן דכתבין שעות, אלא] מה טעמא עבד מר הכי, אמר ליה שודא דדיאני, אנא נמי שודא דדיאני, אמר ליה חדא דאנא דיינא ומר לא דייאנא, ועוד מעיקרא לאו בתורת הכי אתית להו.

והפרטים שבמין זה רבו מלספור.

ד:א:ב - מעשיות שאירעו שיש בהן תועלת במדות

והמין השני - הוא {מעשה} אשר יש ללמוד ממנו תועלת במדות, כמאמרם ז"ל בגמרא שבת[מג] לעולם יהא אדם ענותן כהלל ולא יהא קפדן כשמאי, מעשה בשני בני אדם שהמרו זה את זה [אמרו כל מי שילך ויקניט את הלל יטול ארבע מאות זוז מחבירו, אמר אחד אני אלך, אותו היום ערב שבת היה והיה הלל חופף את

> was the Sabbath eve, and Hillel was washing his head. He (the aggravator) went and stood at the entrance to his (Hillel's) house and said, "Is Hillel here, is Hillel here?" He (Hillel) wrapped himself [in his garments] and went out to greet him. He said to him, "My son, what do you seek?" He (the aggravator) said to him, "I have one question to ask; if only you would answer it." He (Hillel) said to him, "Ask, my son, ask." He (the aggravator) said to him, "Why are the heads of Babylonians not round?" He (Hillel) said to him, "My son, a great question you have asked. It is is because they do not have intelligent midwives." He went and waited for a moment, and returned and said, "Is Hillel here, is Hillel here?" [Once again] He (Hillel) wrapped himself [in his garments] and went out to greet him. He said to him, "My son, what do you seek?" He (the aggravator) said to him, "I have one question to ask; if only you would answer it." He (Hillel) said to him, "Ask, my son, ask." He (the aggravator) said to him, "Why are the eyes of the residents of Tadmor bleary?" He (Hillel) said to him, "My son, a great question you have asked. It is because they live among the sands." [Once again] He went and waited for a moment, and returned and said, "Is Hillel here, is Hillel here?" [Once again] He (Hillel) wrapped himself [in his garments] and went out to greet him. He said to him, "My son, what do you seek?" He (the aggravator) said to him, "I have one question to ask; if only you would answer it." He (Hillel) said to him, "Ask, my son, ask." He (the aggravator) said to him, "Why do Africans have wide feet?" He (Hillel) said to him, "My son, a great question you have asked. It is because they live among the marshes." He (the aggravator) said to him, "Are you Hillel, that they say of you Prince of Israel?" He said to him "Yes." He (the aggravator) said to him, "There should not be more like you in Israel." He (Hillel) said to him, "For what reason?" He (the aggravator) said to him, "For you caused me to lose four hundred *zuz*." He (Hillel) said to him, "My son, be vigilant [from entering into these bets], for Hillel is capable of causing you to lose four hundred *zuz*, and four hundred *zuz* more, and Hillel will not be upset."

From this narrative we learn a very valuable moral lesson; namely, one must emulate Hillel, peace be upon him, in compassion and averseness to anger – even regarding matters which may cause great anger (as in this [above] narrative). Narratives of a similar type are abundant in the Talmud.

ראשו, הלך ועמד על פתח ביתו אמר מי כן בי הלל מי בי הלל, נתעטף ויצא לקראתו, אמר לו בני מה אתה מבקש אמר לו שאלה אחת יש לי לשאל ולואי שתשיבני, אמר לו שאל בני שאל, אמר לו מפני מה ראשיהן של בבליים אינו מגולגל, אמר לו בני שאלה גדולה שאלת מפני שאין להם חיות פקחות. הלך והמתין שעה אחת ובא ואמר מיכן בי הלל מיכן בי הלל, נתעטף ויצא לקראתו, אמר לו בני מה אתה מבקש, אמר לו שאלה אחת יש לי לשאל ולואי שתשיבני, אמר לו שאל בני שאל, אמר לו מפני מה עיניהן של תדמוריין תרוטות, אמר לו בני שאלה גדולה שאלת מפני שהן דרין בין החולות. הלך והמתין שעה אחת חזר ואמר מיכן בי הלל מיכן בי הלל, נתעטף ויצא לקראתו, אמר לו בני מה אתה מבקש, אמר לו שאלה אחת יש לי לשאל ולואי שתשיבני, אמר לו שאל בני שאל, אמר לו מפני מה רגליהם שלאפרקיים רחבות, אמר לו בני שאלה גדולה שאלת מפני שדרים בין בצעי המים. אמר לו אנת הוא הלל שאומרין עליך נשיא ישראל, אמר לו הין, אמר לו כמותך אל ירבו בישראל, אמר לו מפני מה, אמר לו שאבדת ממני ארבע מאות זוז, אמר לו בני הזהר ברוחך כדי הוא הלל שיאבד ממך ארבע מאות זוז וארבע מאות זוז] והלל אל יקניט.

ממעשה זה למדים מידה מוסרית רבת ערך, והיא שצריך {אדם} להידמות להלל ע"ה באריכת אפיים וההמנעות מהכעס - ואפילו על דברים המכעיסים מאד [כמו הענין הזה שספרוהו]. וכעין זה הסוג יש בתלמוד הרבה.

4:1:3 Narratives which Contain Virtues of Faith

The third type [in this category] is that of the narrative from which we may learn proper faith, as is mentioned in the *Mishna* of *Ta'anit:*[1]

> **It once happened that they told Ḥoni the Encircler** [to pray] **that rain should fall. He said to them, "Go out and bring in the** [clay] **ovens of Passover in order that they do not dissolve." He prayed, and they (the rains) did not fall. He drew a circle and stood in it, and said, "Master of the World, Your children have turned their faces toward me, for I am like a member of Your household before you. I swear by Your great name that I will not move from here until You have mercy upon Your children." Rain began to fall softly. He said, "I did not ask for this, but for rains of cisterns, ditches, and caves." They (the rains) began to fall intensely. He said, "I did not ask for this, but for rains of benevolence, blessing, and generosity." They (the rains) then fell properly.**

From this story one learn proper faith; namely, that God, may He be blessed and may His name be exalted, answers the prayers of His righteous servants, as His Torah established: *For what great nation is there that has God so close to it, as is the Lord our God [Who is so close to Israel] whenever we call upon Him?*[2] And it is said by His Prophet: *Then, you shall call, and the Lord will answer; you shall cry out, and He shall say 'Here I am'...*[3] In Moses' prayer: *He shall call to me, and I shall answer Him.*[4, 5]

---

1 3:8

2 Deuteronomy 4:7

3 Isaiah 58:9

4 Psalms 91:15

5 The Divine providence one experiences is dependent on one's own self-perfection. HaRaMBa"M writes (*Guide* III, 18):

> [The revelation of] Divine Providence is therefore not the same to all men; the greater the human perfection a person has attained, the greater the benefit he derives from Divine Providence. This benefit is very great in the case of prophets, and varies according to the degree of their prophetic faculty, as it varies in the case of pious and good men according to

והמין השלישי - הוא המעשה שנלמד ממנו אמונה נכונה, כמו שאמר במשנת תעניות[מג] מעשה שאמרו לו לחוני המעגל {התפלל} שירדו גשמים, אמר להן צאו והכניסו תנורי פסחים בשביל שלא ימוקו, התפלל ולא ירדו, עג עוגה ועמד בתוכה ואמר רבונו של עולם בניך שמים פניהם עלי [שאני כבן בית לפניך, נשבע אני בשמך הגדול שאיני זז מכאן עד שתרחם על בניך, התחילו גשמים מנטפין אמר לא כך שאלתי אלא גשמי בורות שיחין ומערות, ירדו בזעף אמר לא כך שאלתי אלא גשמי רצון ברכה ונדבה, ירדו כתיקנן].

הנה יש ללמוד מהמעשה הזה אמונה נכונה, והיא שהשם יתברך ויתעלה שמו עונה לתפלת עבדיו הצדיקים, כמו שכללה תורתו[מד] ומי גוי גדול אשר לו אלהים קרובים אליו כה' אלהינו [בכל קראינו אליו], ונאמר על ידי נביאו[מה] אז תקרא וה' יענה [תשוע ויאמר הנני], ובתוך מה שכללתו תפלת משה[מו] יקראני ואענהו.

A similar passage is found in *Ta'anit*:[1]

> **It once happened that all of Israel ascended for the** [festive] **pilgrimage, and there was no water for them to drink. Naqdimon ben Gurion went to a certain officer who was there and said to him, "Lend me twelve wells of water and** [if I cannot return the water] **I will give you twelve talents of silver." He agreed to the price and set him a time. When the time arrived and the rains had not fallen, he (the officer) sent a message to him: "Send me either the water or the money." He (Naqdimon) sent a message to him: "I still have time." At noontime he (the officer) sent him a message: "Send me either the water or the money." He (Naqdimon) sent a message to him: "I still have time left in the day." In the afternoon he (the officer) sent him a message: "Send me either the water or the money." He (Naqdimon) sent him a message: "I still have time left in the day." The officer said, "For the entire year rain has not fallen, and now** [you expect] **it will rain?!" He (the officer) entered the bathhouse** [in a state of joy]. **What did he** [Naqdimon] [then] **do?**[2] **Naqdimon entered the Temple in a state of sadness. He wrapped himself** [in a prayer shawl] **and stood in prayer,** [and] **said before Him, "Master of the World, it is revealed and known before You that I did not act for my own honour, nor did I act for the honour of my father's house. Rather, I acted for Your honour, in order that there should be abundant water for the pilgrims." Immediately the sky was filled with clouds, and rains fell until the twelve cisterns were filled with water, and** [even] **overflowed...He (the officer) said to him, "I know that the Holy One, Blessed be He, has shaken His world only for you. However, I still have a claim against you, by which I can take my money from you, for the sun had already set, and** [thus] **the rains fell under my prerogative. He (Naqdimon) returned to the Temple, wrapped himself** [in a prayer shawl], **and stood in prayer, saying before Him, "Master of the World, let it be known that You have**

their piety and uprightness...In the same proportion as ignorant and disobedient persons are deficient in that Divine influence, their condition is inferior, and their rank equal to that of irrational beings; and they are "like the beasts" (Psalms 49:21)... The protection of the pious by Providence is also expressed in the following passages... "The eyes of the Lord are upon the righteous" (Psalms 49:16); "He shall call upon me and I shall answer him" (Psalms 91:15). There are, in Scripture, many more passages expressing the principle that men enjoy Divine protection in proportion to their perfection and piety.

1 19b-20a

2 The remaining segment is added for the reader's convenience.

וכיוצא בזה בתלמוד אומרם בגמ' תעניות[מז] פעם אחת עלו כל ישראל לרגל ולא היה להם מים לשתות, הלך נקדימון בן גריון [אצל הגמון אחד שהיה שם, אמר לו הלויני שתים עשרה מעלות מים ואני נותן לך שנים עשר ככרי כסף, קצץ לו כסף וקבע לו זמן. כשהגיע זמנו ולא ירדו גשמים, שלח לו שגר לי או מים או מעות, שלח לו עד אן יש לו רוח, בצהרים שלח לו שגר לי או מים או מעות, שלח לו עד אן יש לי שהות ביום. במנחה שלח לו שגר לי או מים או מעות, שלח לו עד אן יש לי שהות ביום. אמר אותו הגמון כל השנה כולה לא ירדו גשמים ועכשיו ירדו, נכנס לבית המרחץ. מה עשה] נקדימון נכנס לבית המקדש כשהוא עצב נתעטף ועמד בתפלה אמר לפניו רבונו של עולם גלוי וידוע לפניך שלא לכבודי עשיתי ולא לכבוד בית אבא עשיתי אלא לכבודך עשיתי שיהו מים מצויין לעולי רגלים, מיד נתקשרו שמים בעבים וירדו גשמים עד שנתמלאו שתים עשרה מעינות מים והותירו וכו' אמר לו יודע אני שלא הרעיש הקדוש ברוך הוא את עולמו אלא בשבילך אלא עדיין יש לי פתחון פה עליך שאוציא ממך את מעותיי שכבר שקעה חמה וגשמים ברשותי ירדו, חזר ונכנס לבית המקדש נתעטף ועמד בתפלה ואמר לפניו רבונו של עולם הודע שיש לך אהובים

> **beloved ones in Your world." Immediately, the clouds scattered and the sun shone...It was taught: Naqdimon was not his name, but rather his name was Buni; why is he called Naqdimon? because the sun broke through [*Naqda*] on his behalf.**

Many similar narratives are found in the Talmud.

4:1:4 Narratives which Relate Improbable Occurrences

The fourth type [in this category] are recorded narratives in which wonders and bafflements occurred.[1] An example of this is the [following] passage in *Yoma*:[2]

> **Ribbi Meir and Ribbi Yehuda and Ribbi Jose were walking on the road. They arrived at a certain inn. Ribbi Meir said to the innkeeper, "My son, what is your name?" He said to them, "Kidor." They (the other rabbis) entrusted their purses to him, but Ribbi Meir did not entrust his purse to him;**[3] [instead] **Ribbi Meir placed it at the grave of his (the innkeeper's) father. He (the innkeeper's father) appeared to him (the innkeeper) in a dream** [and said]: **"Go take the purse placed at the head of that man (the innkeeper's father)." The following day, he (the innkeeper) said to them (the rabbis), "This** [is what] **appeared to me in my dream..." They (the rabbis) said to him, "Dreams during twilight have no substance** [and should not be given credence]. [Even so,] **Ribbi Meir went and guarded** [his purse] **all that day and then took it** [back]. **The following day, they (the rabbis) said to him (the innkeeper), "Give us our purses." He said to them, "These matters never occurred** [you never entrusted me with your purses]. **Ribbi Meir said to them, "Why did you not analyse his name** [to learn that he is a wicked man]?"[4] **They said to him, "Why did the Master not tell us** [that he is an evil man]?" **He said to them, "I said that I suspect him, but did I say he should be established as such?"**

1 As mentioned above, these narratives were recorded because of their connection to a matter previously discussed. They were also recorded to demonstrate the greatness of certain scholars, as will be explained.

2 83b

3 The remaining segment is added for the reader's convenience.

4 The standard Vilna edition includes Ribbi Meir's analysis of Kidor's name at the time when he inquired it of him: "He said, 'Learn from this that he is an evil man, as the verse states, "for they are a generation (*ki dor*) of turmoils" (Deuteronomy 32:20)'"

בעולמך, מיד נתפזרו העבים וזרחה החמה וכו' תנא לא נקדימון שמו אלא בוני שמו ו]לפיכך נקרא שמו נקדימון שנקדה לו חמה בעבורו. וכמוהו הרבה בתלמוד.

ד:א:ד - מעשיות בלתי שכיחות שאירעו

המין הרביעי - מעשיות שנכתבו מפני שאירע בהם דבר פלא וענין תימה. וכמוהו מה שאמר ביומא[מח] ר' מאיר ור' יהודה ור' יוסי הוו קאזלי באורחא איקלעו לההיא אושפיזא א"ל ר' מאיר לאושפיזא בני מה שמך, א"ל כידור. אינהו יהבו ליה כיסייהו ור' מאיר לא יהיב ליה כיסיה וכו'.

This story was written solely in order to inform you of Ribbi Meir's comprehension, and the extraordinary event which proved Ribbi Meir's assumptions in recognizing such an individual.

A similar passage is found in *Megila*:[1]

> **Ribbi Yehuda Nesiah sent the leg of a third** [-born] **calf and a jug of wine to Ribbi Oshạyah. He (Ribbi Oshạyah) sent** [the following message] **to him: "You have fulfilled through us, our teacher,** [the Purim *miṣva* of] **'gifts to the poor.'**[2] **He (Ribbi Yehuda Nesiah) then sent him the kidney of a third** [-born] **calf and three jugs of wine. He (Ribbi Oshạyah) sent** [the following message] **to him: "You have fulfilled through us, our teacher,** [the Purim *miṣva* of] **'sending portions from a man to his friend.'**[3]

And the same is so for similar [narratives]. Narratives of this type are abundant in the Talmud, especially in tractate *Giṭin*[4] and elsewhere.

It is possible that varied explanations of these narratives may cause other benefits to be extracted from them, and thus [cause them to] be included within [any of] the three earlier types which we have already discussed. The truth, however, is that these narratives remain of a separate, fourth type, as we have explained.

4:2 Narratives which did not Occur in Reality, Rather in a Dream

The second category is comprised of narratives which were seen and which occurred in dreams; these were related [by the Sages] in an ordinary fashion,[5] for it was obvious to them that an intelligent person would

1 7a

2 Esther 9:22

3 Ibid. It is unclear why Rabbenu Avraham placed this story within the fourth subcategory and not the first, as it seems to instruct in matters of *halakha* (e.g. which items may be used for *Mishloaḥ Manot*), and not in extraordinary matters.

4 Perhaps Rabbenu Avraham is referring to the stories regarding the destruction of the Temple (*Giṭin* 55b–58a), as they are manifestly stories of extraordinary matters.

5 As if they actually took place in real life.

הנה המעשה הזה לא נכתב אלא להודיעך בינת ר' מאיר, והפלא שאירע {במה} שנתאמתו דברי ר' מאיר בהכרת האיש ההוא.

וכמוהו מה שאמר במגילה[מט] דר' יהודה נשיאה שלח ליה לר' אושעיה אטמא דעגלא תלתא וגרבא דחמרא, שלח ליה קיימת בנו רבנו מתנות לאביונים, הדר שלח ליה כוליא דעגלא תלתא ותלתא גרבי דחמרא, שלח ליה קיימת בנו רבינו ומשלוח מנות איש לרעהו. וכן כל כיוצא בזה.

ומעשיות בדרך הזה בתלמוד לאין מספר, ובגמרא דגיטין תמצא מהן לרוב, ו{כן} במקומות אחרים בתלמוד.

ואפשר כי בהתחלק דיעות המפרשים ב{ביאור} מעשיות אלו {יתכן} שימצא בהם תועלות אחרות, וימצאו {שהם נכללים} בשלשת הדרכים שדברנו בהם כבר. ו{אמנם} האמת {היא} שזה החלק מהמעשיות יש לו דרך רביעי בפני עצמו על הדרך שבארנו.

ד:ב - מעשיות שלא נתרחשו במציאות אלא בחלום

החלק השני - המעשיות שנראו וארעו להם בחלום, וזכרו אותם בלשון צח ופשוט לדעתם, כי אי איפשר

not err [and interpret them literally]. An example of this is the passage in *Berakhot*:[1]

> **It was taught** in a *beraita*: **Ribbi Ishmael** said, **"I once entered the innermost sanctum to offer incense,**[2] **and I saw Akatriel Yah, Lord of Hosts, seated upon a high and exalted throne. He said to me, 'Ishmael, My son, bless Me.' I said to Him, 'May it be Your will that Your mercy overcome Your anger, and may Your mercy prevail over Your** [other] **attributes, and may You act with Your children in the attribute of mercy, and may You enter for them beyond the letter of the law.' He nodded His head."**[3]

The Sages' words are filled with other similar narratives. And the same is true regarding narratives recalling visions of prophets, [which relate that angels] spoke to them and assisted them.[4] The same is true

1 7a

2 The remaining segment is added for the reader's convenience.

3 See Rabbenu Ḥananel's comments to the above passage: "Some are of the opinion that Akatriel is an angel; we, however, have received through tradition that it refers to God."

Rabbenu Avraham interprets this story to be a dream since physical attributes are being given to a spiritual being. For even if he is of the opinion that Akatriel refers to an angel, it is most probable that he would not deviate from his father's opinion that interactions with angels only occur through visions (see *Guide* II, 42):

> We have already shown that the appearance or speech of an angel mentioned in Scripture took place in a vision or dream; it makes no difference whether this is expressly stated or not, as we have explained above.

This is congruent with HaRaMBa"M's opinion that angels are incorporeal (*MT, Yesodei HaTorah* 2:3):

> Everything which the Holy One, blessed be He, created within His world is divided into three categories. They include…Creations which have form, but no matter at all; for example, the angels, for the angels do not possess bodies or corporeal being, but rather are forms which are separate from each other.

4 This follows HaRaMBa"M's approach (*MT, Yesodei HaTorah* 7:6): "[Divine insight is bestowed upon] all the Prophets (except for Moses) through the medium of an angel. Therefore, they perceive only metaphoric imagery and allegories."

This reading is based on R. Moshe Maimon's rendition, as can be seen in the added Hebrew text inside the braces. However, it is my opinion that these added words are unnecessary, as it is possible that Rabbenu Avraham is referring to the many narratives in which prophets appear to *Tannaim* or *Amoraim*, offering them insights. This can be seen from the many stories of Eliyahu haNavi in the Talmud. See *Qoveṣ*

שיטעה בהם בעל שכל ובינה. וכמוהו מה שאמרו חז"ל בברכות׳ **תניא אמר ר' ישמעאל פעם אחת נכנסתי להקטיר קטורת לפני ולפנים** {וראיתי אכתריאל} **וכו'.**

וכזה נמצא בדבריהם בהרבה מקומות. וכמו כן **במעשיות שזוכרין בהם מראות הנביאים ו** {שזוכרין מה} **שדברו עמהם ו** {מה} **שהועילו עמהם** {המלאכים}**.** **וכמו** {כן} **מעשיות שזכרו בהם שדים.**

regarding narratives which mention demons.[1]

A thoughtless person who sees these [narratives in the Talmud] will think that they were actual occurrences – just as they were written, and will come to contemplate and believe that matters which are contrary [to logic] are possible or [even] inevitable. All this shall happen to him due to the extent of his foolishness and lack of knowledge in natural sciences,[2] and [due to a misunderstanding of] miracles and the [literary] style of the Sages, of blessed memory – which is the style of the Prophets, who related, in simple speech, that which they saw in prophetic visions. This path was trod by the Sages, as my father and master, of blessed memory, explained in the *Guide for the Perplexed*, for those who understand.[3]

Teshuvot HaRaMBa"M, (1859) *Pirqe HaHaṣlaḥah* 4, where HaRaMBa"M writes that Eliyahu haNavi passed away without any surviving trace of a physical body. Thus, all narratives of Eliyahu mentioned in the Talmud perforce transpired in visions or dreams.

1 Although the simple reading of many passages in the Talmud might imply that the Sages believed demons to be actual physical entities (see, for example, *Ḥagiga* 16a, *Giṭin* 66a, *Berakhot* 3a), Rabbenu Avraham interprets them to be descriptions and accounts which take place within dreams. Similarly, in *HaMaspiq LeʿOvde HaShem* (*HaShimush BeḤeleq HaDimyoni* [ed. Feldheim, p. 261]) the belief in physical demons is regarded as foolishness and is compared to insanity and mental illness.

Regarding HaRaMBa"M's view on demons, see Rabbi Yosef Qafiḥ's work in "*Ketavim*" (Jerusalem 1989, II, p. 600–601) which demonstrates that HaRaMBa"M did not subscribe to the belief in physical demons.

2 Ibn Ezra (*Yesod Mora VeSod Torah*, ed. Mossad HaRav Kook, Gate I, p. 45) discusses the need to know logic and science in order to interpret both the words of the Torah and those of the Sages adequately.

3 HaRaMBa"M writes (*Guide*, Introduction):

> This second objective included in this work seeks to explain certain obscure parables which occur in the Prophets, and are not distinctly characterised as being parables. Ignorant and superficial readers take them in a literal, not in a figurative sense. Even well-informed persons are bewildered if they understand these passages in their literal signification, but they are entirely relieved of their perplexity when we explain the figure, or merely suggest that the terms are figurative. For this reason, I have called this book Guide for the Perplexed.

He later writes: "Our Sages, imitating the method of Scripture, speak of them (matters relating to creation) in metaphors and allegories."

והרואה {דברים אלו בתלמוד} שאין לבו עמו יחשוב כי הם דברים {ש}היו בעולם כמו שנכתבו, ויבוא לחשוב ולהאמין דבר הנמנע שהוא אפשרי או חייב. וכל זה יקרה לו לרוב פתיותו, ומיעוט ידיעתו בטבע העולם ובמעשה הנסים ובדרך החכמים ז"ל - שהוא דרך הנביאים שספרו בלשון הפשוט מה שראו במראות הנבואה. ודרך זו דרכו {בה} החכמים כמו שביאר אבא מרי ז"ל במורה הנבוכים למבין.

4:3 Narratives which Occurred in Reality, but were Exaggerated

The third category refers to narratives that transpired in the manner in which they were written, but were spoken of in a manner of exaggeration based upon the assumption that one who possesses intelligence would not misinterpret them – for they would recognize and understand that they are [related in] exaggerated speech. An example of this is that which is found in *Tamid*:[1]

> **The Torah spoke in an exaggerated language, the Prophets spoke in an exaggerated language, the Sages spoke in an exaggerated language. The Torah spoke in an exaggerated language** – *great cities and citadels fortified up to the heavens.*[2] **The Prophets spoke in an exaggerated language** – ***the earth was split open by the uproar.***[3] **The Sages spoke in an exaggerated language** – [when they spoke about] **the heap** [of ashes on the altar], **the vine** [which stood at the entrance of the Temple], **and the curtain** [which separated the Holy of Holies from the *Hekhal*].[4]

These three items (the heap, the vine, and the curtain) are discussed in the Mishna, for in the Talmud innumerable exaggeration can be found.

An example of this category is that which was stated in tractate Megila:[5]

> **Rabbah and Ribbi Zera made a [Purim] feast together... Rabbah arose and slaughtered Ribbi Zera... He prayed for mercy upon him, and revived him.**

Its explanation is that he struck him with a great strike, causing him a significant wound, to the point where he was in danger of death. Due to the greatness of this strike, it was stated that he slaughtered him; perhaps it was aimed at the neck. The explanation of "he

1 29a

2 Deuteronomy 9:1

3 I Kings 1:40

4 Thus, the Sages imitated the linguistic style of the Torah and the Prophets. See *Guide*, II, 47 for a further elaboration of this style.

5 7b

ד:ג - מעשיות שאירעו במציאות אלא שהגזימו בסיפורן

החלק השלישי - מעשיות שאירעו בעולם כמו שכתוב בהם, אלא שדברו בהם לשון הבאי לדעתם כי לא יטעה בעל שכל בהם כי הם מכירים ומבינים בהם שהם לשון הבאי. {והוא} כמו שאמרו בגמ' תמיד[כא] **דברה תורה לשון הבאי, דברו נביאים בלשון הבאי, דברו חכמים בלשון הבאי. דברה תורה בלשון הבאי - ערים גדולות ובצורות בשמים, דברו נביאים בלשון הבאי - ותבקע הארץ לקולם, דברו חכמים בלשון הבאי - תפוח וגפן ופרוכת.** ושלשה מקומות אלו {=תפוח גפן ופרוכת} הם במשנה, כי בתלמוד ימצא הבאי לאין מספר, שלא ימנה כ"ג ולא ב"ג.

ודמיון {=ודוגמת} החלק הזה מה שאמרו בגמרא דמגילה[כב] **רבה ור' זירא עבדי סעודתא בהדי הדדי קם רבה שחטיה לר' זירא בעי רחמי עליה ואחייה.** פירושו שהכהו מכה גדולה ופצע בו חבורה גדולה {עד} שנטה למות, ולגודל המכה ההיא קורהו {בלשון} **שחטיה,** ואולי {אמר כן מפני ש}היתה המכה ההיא בצואר. ופירוש **ואחייה** מלשון[כג] {הכתוב} **ויחי**

revived him" is [that it comes from] the [Biblical] language *and he recovered from his illness*,[1] or, in the language of the Sages,[2] "until the wound heals."

A similar passage is found in *Ketubot*:[3]

> **Ribbi Ḥanina bar Ḥakhinai left to the house of study hall at the end of Ribbi Shimon ben Yoḥai's wedding feast. He (Ribbi Shimon) said to him, "Wait for me until I can come with you." He did not wait** for him, **and went and sat in the house of study for ten years. By the time he returned, the paths of his city had changed and he did not know how to go to his home.**
>
> **He went** and **sat on the bank of the river. He heard a certain girl being called to: "Daughter of Ḥakhinai, daughter of Ḥakhinai, fill your pitcher and come, and we will go." He said, "From this I can conclude that this daughter is ours." He followed her** [to his house]. **His wife was sitting and sifting flour. She lifted her eyes up, saw him, and recognized him, and her spirit departed. He said before Him (God): "Master of the World, did this wretch wait for nothing?" He pleaded for mercy upon her and she was revived.**

The explanation of "her spirit departed" is not that the breath of life left her and she [actually] passed away, rather [it means that] out of her great joy in seeing her husband suddenly and unexpectedly, she fell, and part of her living spirit left her [and she fainted], as does happen to individuals at times. He then pleaded for mercy and she was revived and her spirit returned. And so [is the proper approach to] any similar [narrative].[4]

1 Isaiah 38:9

2 *Ketubot* 6a

3 62b

4 Rabbenu Avraham would most likely interpret the beginning of the story to be exaggerated as well, as it is implausible that Ribbi Ḥanina ben Ḥakhinai would be lost in the study hall for such a long time. Nevertheless, his focus was to bring another example of death and resurrection used in a hyperbolic fashion. See R. Margaliot (p. 95, note 71) for more examples of this.

מחליו, ובלשון חכמים ז"ל[יד] עד שתחיה המכה.

וכמוהו {מה שאמרו} **בכתובות[יה] רבי חנינא בר חכינאי הוה קאזיל לבי רב בשילהי הילולא דר' שמעון בן יוחאי (וכו') [אמר ליה איעכב לי עד דאתי בהדך לא איעכבא ליה], ואזיל ויתיב בבי מדרשא עשר שנין (וכו' עד) [עד דאתי אישתנו שבילי דמתא ולא ידע למיזל לביתיה אזל יתיב אגודא דנהרא שמע להיא רביתא דהוו קרו לה בת חכינאי בת חכינאי מלי קולתך ותא ניזיל אמר שמע מינה האי רביתא דידן אזל בתרה הוה יתיבא דביתהו קא נהלה קמחא דל עינה חזיתיה סוי לבה] פרחה רוחה, אמר לפניו רבש"ע ענייה זו לשוא שמרה, בעי רחמי עלה ואחיה.**

ואין פירוש פרחה רוחה שנפרדה ממנה נשמת רוח חיים במיתה, אלא {ש}**מרוב שמחתה כשראתה אותו בפתע פתאום, נפלה ופרח חלק מחלקי הנפש החיה** {ונתעלפה} **כאשר יקרה לבני אדם לפעמים, וביקש רחמים וחיתה ותשב נפשה. וכן כל כיוצא בזה.**

4:4 Narratives which Occurred in Reality, but were Related as Allegories and Riddles

The fourth category includes narratives which indeed occurred, but were related in the form of a parable or riddle, as if it was fashioned in such a manner so that it would not be understood [immediately] by every person. [Rather,] the intent will only be understood and known when he contemplates the form used by this wise and astute individual (that is to say: the author).

We will find, in the plain understanding of narratives of this category, nice and pleasant matters, as well as other matters which will be noticeably inconceivable, even to a simpleton or child. It [may] occur that [even] one who is aware of the impossibility of these matters in their simple understanding will come to believe a certain exegesis according to its simple meaning despite his recognition of its impossibility.[1] However, one who grasps the natural sciences of this world and their manifestations will understand and recognize the matter of the parable or riddle.[2] An example of this is the passage in tractate *Sukka*:[3]

> **There were these two Cushites who would stand before Solomon: Eliḥoreph and Aḥiyah, sons of Shisha, scribes of Solomon. One day he (Solomon) saw that the Angel of Death was distraught. He said to him, "Why are you distraught?" He (the Angel of Death) said to him, "They are asking of me** [to take the lives of] **these two Cushites who are sitting here." He (Solomon) handed them to the demons and sent them to the district of Luz. When they arrived at the district of Luz, they died.**
>
> **The following day, he (Solomon) saw that the Angel of Death was cheerful. He said to him, "Why are you cheerful?" He said to him, "In the place that they asked me** [to take them], **there you**

1 Credence toward a given doctrine may cause scepticism to be completely suppressed.

2 One who is well-educated in the sciences would not have suppressed anything, as it would be obvious that a given passage cannot be taken literally.

3 53a

ד:ד - מעשיות שאירעו במציאות אלא שסיפרו אותן במשל וחידה

החלק הרביעי - הם מעשיות שאירעו באמת, אלא שדברו אותם בתבנית משל וחידה, כאילו נתבונן שלא יתבאר ענינם לכל אדם בכללו, עד {ל} כשיתבונן בצורת מעשה החכם והנבון, יבינהו וידע כוונתו. ויראה בפשט {קצת} מעשיות החלק הזה דברים נאים ונחמדים, ו{כמו כן יראה בקצת מעשיות החלק הזה} דברים אחרים שמניעתם ניכרת אפילו לפתי וקטן. ו{לפעמים} יקרה למי שמניעת דברים אלו בענין פשוטה {שיבא} להאמין הדרש ההוא על פי פשוטו אע"פ שהוא נמנע אצלו. ו{אמנם} למי שידע טבע העולם ודרך מציאותיו {ומבין דרך חז"ל לדבר במשל וחידה, הוא} יבין ענין המשל והחידה ויכירנו.

ודמיון דבר זה כמו שאמרו במס' סוכה" הנהו תרתי כושאי דהוו קיימו קמיה דשלמה, אליחרף ואחיה בני שישא ספרי דשלמה, חזייה למלאך המות דהוה עציב (וכו' עד) [אמר ליה אמאי עציבת אמר ליה דקא בעו מינאי הני תרתי כושאי דיתבי הכא מסרינהו לשעירים שדרינהו למחוזא דלוז כי מטו למחוזא דלוז שכיבו, למחר חזיא מלאך המות דהוה קבדח אמר ליה אמאי בדיחת אמר ליה באתר דבעו מינאי תמן שדרתינהו, מיד] פתח

sent them." Immediately Solomon began to speak, saying "The feet of a person are responsible for him; to the place where he is demanded, there they lead him."

The simple understanding of this story is entirely inconceivable for any individual who possesses intelligence and wisdom.[1] In my opinion, [a version of] this story indeed occurred. Meaning, it became known to Solomon that two [Cushites] were traveling across the world due to a sickness that inhabited them or due to some other matter. He (Solomon) desired to create a scheme to save them from death, and thus had them flee from their current location to another land which was beneficial for them according to their needs and makeup, as he believed that they would be saved there. However, they died in that place – where Solomon believed they would be saved, by the will of God, may He be blessed, before Whom there is no escape or flight. Regarding this, Solomon said "The feet of a person are responsible for him; to the place where he is demanded, there they lead him."

Everything else mentioned in this narrative, besides what we explained, is [present] for the embellishment of the parable and the creation of the riddle.[2] [Alternatively] it is possible that when one closely contemplates the words used in this narrative, one will discover an insight for each and every word.[3] [But] I do not wish to be lengthy with this at the moment.

1 It is inconceivable, since the Angel of Death is not a specific individual, but rather a manifestation of the human condition. As the Gemara states: "Satan, the Evil Inclination, and the Angel of Death are the same..." (*Bava Batra* 16a). See HaRaMBa"M (*Guide* III, 22) for further elucidation.

2 For example, Rabbenu Avraham did not explain why the Angel of Death was sad and then happy, or why demons escorted the Cushites to Luz.

3 HaRaMBa"M describes these two approaches for interpreting the words of the Prophets (*Guide*, Introduction):

> Know that the figures employed by Prophets are of two kinds: first, where every word which occurs in the parable represents a certain idea; and secondly, where the parable, as a whole, represents a general idea, but has a great many points which have no reference whatever to that idea; they are simply required to give to the parable its proper form and order, or better to conceal the idea: the parable is therefore extended as far as is fitting, according to its literal sense. Consider this well.

שלמה ואמר רגלוהי דבר איניש אינון ערבין ביה, לאתר דמתבעיין אינון מובלין ליה.

הנה פשט המעשה נמנע מניעה גמורה לכל בעל שכל ובינה. ועניינו לפי הנראה בעיני הוא דבר אירע באמת, ר"ל כי שני האלה נודע לשלמה כי היו הולכים בדרך כל הארץ מפני חולי שקרה להם או ענין אחר, ורצה לקנות תחבולות להצילם מן המות, והבריחם מן הארץ ההיא אל ארץ אחרת שהיתה טובה להם לפי מה שהיו צריכים ולפי מזגם, שהיה חושב כי ימלטו שם. ו{אמנם} מתו במקום ההוא - אשר חשב שלמה כי שם ימלטו - ברצון השי"ת אשר אין מלפניו לא מנוס ולא מברח, ובזה אמר שלמה **רגלוהי דבר אינש וכו'.**

וכל מה שנאמר בענין המעשה ההוא מלבד מה שפירשנו הוא לתיקון המשל ולחיבור ענין החידה. ואפשר {ש}כשיתבונן אדם היטב במלות המעשה הזה ימצא ענין לכל מלה ומלה, ואין רצוני להאריך עתה בזה.

Do not be surprised that the Sages, of blessed memory, relate stories and legends entirely as parables and riddles, which are not to be taken literally, for they [themselves], of blessed memory, explain verses of the words of the Prophets in this [very same] manner.

See their statements regarding the verse *he went down and struck the lion*[1] and in that [same] verse *he struck down the two strong lions*[2] in *Berakhot*.[3] For they removed it from its simple meaning, despite the Prophets relating it in a simple language, as if there was no other explanation of it. And their intention is not to say that these verses retain an explanation alternative to the simple one, and these are placed in the form of a parable and riddle.[4] All the more so should we enact this approach to their words, whose simple meanings are unfeasible to any who can see with his eyes (that is to say: an honest student).[5] My father and master, of blessed memory, already noted this in his *Commentary to the Mishna*, in the [tenth] chapter [of *Sanhedrin*, known as] *Ḥeleq*.[6]

We have found a notable teaching from them, of blessed memory, which instructs and portrays that riddles and allegories are found

1 II Samuel 23:20; I Chronicles 11:22

2 ibid.

3 18a

4 The Sages do not intend to state that a second explanation exists aside from a correct, simple reading. Rather, they intend that this parable is the only correct meaning, and that to believe the simple meaning would be a mistake.

5 Meaning: If the Prophets' simple words are taken as allegories, then all the more so should the Sages' words be understood as allegories when they are presented in a mysterious way.

6 There HaRaMBa"M writes:

> And how can we blame them (the Sages) for writing wisdom in the way of parable and making it appear as lower things of the masses, when we see that the wisest of all men did this with the holy spirit - I mean Solomon, in Proverbs and in the Song of Songs and in some of Ecclesiastes? And why should it be difficult for us to explain their words rationally and to take them out of their simple meaning in order that they fit reason and correspond to the truth? And even if they are holy writings, they themselves explain verses of Scripture rationally and take them out of their simple meaning and make them into parables.

ואל תתמה מפני שזוכרים החכמים ז"ל בדבריהם מעשיות ואגדות שכולם בכללם משלים וחידות, ואינם על פי פשוטם, שהרי הם ז"ל מפרשים פסוקים מדברי הנביאים על דרך זה. ראה מה שאומרים בפסוק[יז] {ו}הוא {ירד ו}**הכה את הארי**, ובפסוק[יח] **הוא הכה את שני אריאל** בגמרא דברכות,[יט] והוציאוהו מפשוטו עם היות הנביאים אומרים אותו בלשון פשוט כאלו אין בו ענין שני - ואין (רצוני) [רצונם] לומר כי פסוקים אלו יש להם עכ"פ פי' אחר חוץ מפשוטם - ושמים אותם חידות ומשלים. כ"ש שיש לנו לנהוג מנהג זה בדבריהם, שפשוטם נמנע בעיני כל רואה בעיניו. וכבר העיר על זה אבא מרי ז"ל בפרק חלק מפירוש המשנה.

ומצאנו להם ז"ל מאמר נכבד מורה ומודיע כי ימצא חידות ומשלים ברוב דבריהם, {והוא מה}

throughout the majority of their statements; namely, the [following] passage in *Eruvin*:[1]

> **Ribbi Eliezer had a certain disciple who issued a** halakhic **ruling in his presence. He (Ribbi Eliezer) said to Imma Shelim** [his wife], **"I will be surprised if this** [individual] **lives out his year." He** [indeed] **did not complete his year.**
>
> **She said to him, "Are you a prophet?" He said to her, "I am not a prophet, nor am I the son of a prophet. Rather, such has been passed to me through tradition: Anyone who issues a halakhic ruling in his master's presence is liable to death."**
>
> **Rabbah bar bar Ḥana said [that] Rabbi Yoḥanan said, "That disciple was named Yehuda ben Gurya, and he was three parasangs away from him (Ribbi Eliezer),** his teacher"! [The Gemara implies a question: Is it so severe to issue a halakhic ruling in front of one's teacher that even at such distance he was liable to death?!] [The Gemara answers:] **It (the incident) occurred in his (Ribbi Eliezer's)** [immediate] **presence.** [The Gemara challenges this assertion:] **But he (Rabbah bar bar Ḥana) said that he was three parasangs away from him!** [The Gemara counters:] **And, according to your** [the questioner's] **reasoning** [that the details of the story must relate to the time of the ruling], **why** [mention] **his name and his father's name? Rather, the details were given so that you should not say it was a parable.**

Behold, our approach [has been clarified] for you, that their (the Sages') words contain numerous analogies contrary to their simple meaning.[2] Place this evidence upon your heart, and set your eyes upon it, for it is a notable astonishment and great proof, brought to my attention by a wise scholar.

This final category of narratives is quite similar to the second category of exegeses, in the sense that both of these categories are notable and pleasant, containing great and wondrous concepts, which are not to be revealed to every individual. For this reason,

1 63a

2 Accordingly, in any instance when the details of certain individuals are not defined, one must entertain the possibility that the passage may be an allegory.

שאמרו בגמרא דערובין[ס] תלמיד אחד שהיה לו לר' אליעזר שהורה הלכה לפניו, אמר לה לאימא שלים דביתהו תמיה אני אם יוציא זה שנתו, ולא הוציא שנתו. אמרה לו וכי נביא אתה (וכו' עד) [אמר לה לא נביא אנכי ולא בן נביא אנכי אלא כך מקובלני כל המורה הלכה בפני רבו חייב מיתה ואמר רבה בר בר חנה אמר רבי יוחנן אותו תלמיד יהודה בן גוריא שמו והיה רחוק ממנו שלש פרסאות בפניו הוה והא רחוק ממנו שלש פרסאות קאמר וליטעמיך] שמו ושם אביו למה, שלא תאמר משל היה.

הנה {נתבאר} לך {מה} שהורינו בזה, שיש בדבריהם משלים רבים שאינם על פי פשוטם. והשב ראיה זו על לבך ושים עינך בה, כי היא פליאה נכבדת וראיה גדולה, והעיר אותי על ראיה זו אחד מנבוני תלמידי החכמים.

והחלק הזה האחרון מן המעשיות קרוב להיותו מהחלק השני מהדרשות, ר"ל שהשני חלקים נכבדים וכלם מחמדים ועניניהם גדולים ונפלאים, ואין לגלותם לכל אדם - ומפני זה דרכו בהם דרכי

they (the Sages) trod the paths of riddle and allegory.[1] You must be aware of this.

◆◆◆

1 HaRaMBa"M explains why the Sages did this (*Introduction to the Mishna*, 16):

> And they did this thing for wondrous matters: One of them is to sharpen the ideas of their students and to draw their hearts. They also did this to blind the eyes of fools who will never illuminate their hearts. And if they had shown them the illumination of truths, they [the students] would have turned their faces away from them according to the shortcomings of their natures. As it is stated about them and those similar to them, "We do not reveal the secret to them" – because their intellect is not complete in order to accept the truths with clarity.

החידות והמשלים, ואתה דע לך.

◆◆◆

Chapter 5

Narratives and exegeses assembled from multiple components

One of the matters of which you must be aware and which you should contemplate – for you will have a great aid in understanding the [Sages'] narratives – is that, within a [given] narrative, two or more [elements of the above] categories of narrative may be found. For example, some part of it will have taken place in a dream, and part while awake, and part as allegory or riddle. If you would attempt to explain this entire narrative within the framework of one of these categories, confusion will abound, and the truth of the narrative will remain unknown. Noting this is enough of an aid for you. And know that exegeses will also be found [to be combined]; meaning, one exegesis may contain [elements from] two or more [of the above] categories.

An example of a narrative comprised of [elements from] two or more categories is the following passage in *Ḥagiga*:[1]

> **The Sages taught: It once happened that Rabban Yoḥanan ben Zakai was riding on a donkey, traveling** [away] **from Jerusalem, and Ribbi Elạzar ben Arakh was walking after him to learn Torah from his mouth. He (Ribbi Elạzar) said to him, "My master, teach me one chapter from** [the incident of] **the Divine Chariot (*Ma'ạse Merkava*). He (Rabban Yoḥanan) said to him, "Have I not taught you:** [one may] **not** [expound upon] **the** Divine **Chariot by oneself, unless he is wise and understands of his own accord?" He said to him, "My master, allow me to say before you one matter that you have taught me." He said to him, "Speak."**
>
> **Immediately, Rabban Yoḥanan ben Zakai alighted from the donkey, and wrapped himself** [in his prayer shawl], **and sat on a stone under an olive tree. He (Ribbi Elạzar) said to him, "For what reason did you alight from the donkey?" He (Rabban Yoḥanan) said, "Is it possible that as you expound matters of the Divine Chariot, and the Divine Presence is with us, and the ministering angels are accompanying us, and I should ride upon a donkey?"**

1 14b

פרק ה

מעשיות ודרשות מורכבות מחלקים שונים

ו אחד מן הדברים שיש לך להתעורר ולהתבונן בו מפני שיש לך תועלת גדולה בידיעת המעשיות הוא שתדע כי ימצא במעשה אחד שני חלקים מחלקי המעשיות או יותר, כגון שהיה {חלק} ממנו בחלום ו{חלק} ממנו בהקיץ בלי ספק, ו{חלק} ממנו משל וחידה. וכשתבוא לפרש כל המעשה על דרך חלק אחד מן החלקים תגדל המבוכה, ולא יודע אמיתת המעשה, ולהעירך בזה די לך תועלת. ודע, כי {גם} כן הדרשות נמצאים {מורכבים}, ר"ל כי ימצא דרש אחד מורכב משני חלקים או יותר.

ודמיון המעשה המורכב משני חלקים או יותר {הוא} מה שאמרו בחגיגה[פא] ת"ר מעשה בר' יוחנן בן זכאי שהיה רוכב על החמור ויוצא מירושלים, ור' אליעזר בן ערך מהלך אחריו ללמוד תורה מפיו, א"ל רבי שנה לי פרק אחד במעשה מרכבה, א"ל ולא כך שניתי לכם ולא במרכבה ביחיד אא"כ היה חכם ומבין מדעתו (וכו' עד) [אמר לו רבי תרשיני לומר לפניך דבר אחד ממה שלמדתני, אמר לו אמור, מיד ירד רבן יוחנן בן זכאי מן החמור ונתעטף וישב על האבן תחת הזית, אמר לו {רבי} מפני מה ירדת מן החמור, א"ל אפשר אתה דורש במעשה מרכבה ושכינה עמנו ומלאכי השרת מלוין אותנו ואני רוכב

> **Immediately, Elạzar ben Ạrakh began** [to discuss] **the matter of the Divine Chariot, and expounded upon it. A fire descended from heaven and encircled all the trees in the field, and all** [the trees] **began reciting song.**
>
> **Which song did they recite?** ***Praise the Lord from the earth...***[1] **Some say** [they sang] ***Then shall the trees of the forest sing, "Praise the Lord."***[2] **A response emanated from the fire, stating, "This is** the matter of **the Divine Chariot." Rabban Yoḥanan ben Zakai stood and kissed him on his head, and said, "Blessed be God, Lord of Israel, who gave our father Avraham a son like this one, who knows how to understand, analyse, and expound** the matter of **the Divine Chariot. Some expound well but do not fulfil well, and some fulfil well but do not expound well.** [You] **Elạzar ben Ạrakh expound well and fulfil well. Praiseworthy are you, our father Avraham, that Elạzar ben Ạrakh came from your loins."**

Behold, without a doubt a part of this narrative transpired in reality, as is mentioned,[3] and a part of it in a dream.[4] Thus, it is comprised of [elements from] the first and second categories [of narratives].

An example of a narrative comprised of [elements from] three categories is the narrative which follows the previous one; namely, the following passage from our Sages, of blessed memory:[5]

> **When these matters were related before R. Joshua, he was walking along the way with R. Jose the Priest. They said, "We, too, shall expound upon** the matter of **the Divine Chariot." R. Joshua began expounding upon the matter of the Divine Chariot. That day was the summer solstice, and the heavens became filled with clouds, and the rainbow appeared in a cloud. The minister-**

---

1 Psalms 148:7

2 *Pereq Shira* 3:1

3 There is no reason to doubt that the initial interaction between Rabban Yoḥanan ben Zakai and Ribbi Elạzar ben Ạrakh transpired in waking reality.

4 According to Rabbenu Avraham, the story segmented into the realm of dreams once heavenly fires and singing trees appeared. Perhaps he interprets the fire to represent a transformation into a certain spiritual state.

5 *Ḥagiga* ibid.

על החמור. מיד פתח רבי אלעזר בן ערך במעשה מרכבה ודרש וירדה אש מן השמים וסיבבה את כל האילנות שבשדה, פתחו כולם פיהן ואמרו שירה, ומה שירה אמרו הללו את ה' מן הארץ {וגו'} וי"א אז ירננו עצי היער הללו את ה', ענה {מלאך} מתוך האש ואמר הם הם מעשה המרכבה. עמד רבן יוחנן בן זכאי ונשקו על ראשו ואמר ברוך ה' אלהי ישראל שנתן בן כזה לאברהם אבינו שיודע להבין ולחקור ולדרוש במעשה מרכבה, יש נאה דורש ואין נאה מקיים, ויש נאה מקיים ואין נאה דורש, {אתה} אלעזר בן ערך נאה דורש ונאה מקיים אשריך אברהם אבינו שאלעזר בן ערך] יצא מחלציך.

הנה המעשה הזה קצתו היה בהקיץ בלי ספק כמו שאמר, וקצתו בחלום. נמצא שהוא מורכב מן החלק הראשון ומן השני, וכן כל כיוצא בזה.

ודמיון המעשה המורכב מג' חלקים, {הוא} המעשה שאחר זה המעשה שהזכרנו, וזה שאמרו חז"ל[סג] וכשנאמרו הדברים לפני ר' יהושע (וכו' עד) [היה הוא ורבי יוסי הכהן מהלכין בדרך, אמרו אף אנו נדרוש במעשה מרכבה, פתח רבי יהושע ודרש במעשה מרכבה, ואותו היום היתה תקופת תמוז ונתקשרו שמים בעבים ונראתה הקשת בענן, והיו

> **ing angels gathered and came in the guise of a bridegroom and bride.**
>
> **R. Jose the Priest went and related these matters before Rabban Yoḥanan ben Zakai** [who said], **"Praiseworthy are all of you, praiseworthy are those who birthed you, and praiseworthy is my eye which saw this. I saw myself and you in my dream: We were reclining on Mount Sinai, and a Divine Voice from Heaven was placed upon us** [, stating], **'Ascend to here, ascend to here,** [for there are] **large halls** prepared for you, **pleasant couches spread for you. You, your students, and the students of your students are invited to the third group.**

Behold, a part of this narrative is comprised from [elements of] the first category, and a portion from [elements of] the second category, and a portion from [elements of] the fourth category. The first category is demonstrated in this narrative in the preliminary section of the narrative, when these great men engaged in the exposition of the matter of the Divine Chariot. The second category is demonstrated in Rabban Yoḥanan ben Zakai's statement "I saw...in my dream." The fourth category is demonstrated in what was stated regarding the gathering of angels and their presence before them.[1] It is impossible (that is to say: prohibited) to explain the meaning of this matter, for it would be revealing a secret.

◆◆◆

1 Although this occurred in the dream (the domain of the second category), it is clearly a riddle or allegory, and should therefore be addressed as the domain of the fourth category. This is unlike the previous story, which did not contain a riddle/ allegory within the dream.

מלאכי השרת מתקבצין ובאין במזומי חתן וכלה, הלך רבי יוסי הכהן וסיפר דברים לפני רבן יוחנן בן זכאי {ואמר} אשריכם אשרי יולדתכם ואשרי עיני שכך ראו, ואף אני ואתם {ראיתי} בחלומי היינו מסובין על הר סיני ונתנה עלינו בת קול מן השמים עלו לכאן עלו לכאן מרקליטין גדולים מוכנין לכם מצעות נאות מוצעות {לכם} אתם ותלמידיכם ותלמידי תלמידיכם] מזומנים לכת השלישית.

הנה המעשה קצתו מהחלק הראשון וקצתו מהחלק השני וקצתו מהחלק הרביעי. ודמיון החלק הראשון מהמעשה הזה הוא גוף המעשה הנזכר בראשונה שהיו גבורים אלו מתעסקים בדרוש מעשה המרכבה. ודמיון החלק השני מבואר במה שאמר ר' יוחנן בן זכאי ראיתי בחלומי, ודמיון החלק הרביעי {הוא} מה שאמרו בענין קבוץ המלאכים (ועומדים) [ועמידתם] לפניו. ואי אפשר {לבאר} פירוש ענין זה כי הוא גילוי סוד.

◆◆◆

Chapter 6

Conclusion

We have already spoken [in] much [detail], and have entered inside without permission.[1] We have explained that which is sufficient for every discerning and wise person. I say that in my decomposition of the narratives and exegeses into their categories, and in my presentation of examples for each of these categories, that I have covered all exegeses and narratives found in the Talmud to the closest extent possible for he who understands. For I know that after [all] this, no individual shall find it difficult when he encounters an exegesis or hears a narrative, to know and understand to which of the aforementioned categories it belongs.

Through this, one's soul will be saved from spreading lies against the speakers [of these exegeses and narratives] (meaning: the Sages] of blessed memory, as do the Qaraites, the fools, and the like. Furthermore, [one's soul will be saved] from drowning in the ignorance of the fools who believe the impossible. [For if one were to believe such matters] one will believe that he has found something that does not exist and that something which never occurred indeed did occur.[2]

1 Although Rabbenu Avraham did not reveal actual mysteries [*sodot*], rather the methods for their detection, he felt that he was treading dangerous waters. As HaRaMBa"M writes (*Yesodei HaTorah* 2:12):

> The Sages of the early generations commanded that these matters [*Ma'ase Merkava*] should not be explained except to a single individual at a time. [This individual] should be a wise man, who can reach understanding by using his own knowledge. Afterwards, he is given the fundamental points, with only a few basic concepts made known to him. He will then reach understanding with his powers of knowledge and know the ultimate meaning and depth of the concept.

2 HaRaMBa"M writes about this group (*Commentary to the Mishna, Sanhedrin* 10:1):

> [Regarding] this group of poor-minded ones, one must be pained by their foolishness. As they think that they are honouring and raising the Sages; but in reality they are lowering them to the lowest depths – and they do not understand this.
>
> By God, may He be blessed, Who lives, this group destroys the beauty of the Torah and darkens its splendour, and places the Torah of God opposite that which was intended in it, as God, may He be blessed, said in the perfect Torah (Deuteronomy 4:6), "that they should observe all of these statutes and they (the nations of the world) shall say, 'This is certainly a wise and understanding people, this great nation.'" This group recounts the statements of

פרק ו - סיום

ו ככבר דברנו גדולות, ונכנסנו לפנים שלא ברשות, וביארנו מה שיש בו סיפוק לכל נבון וחכם. ואומר אני כי בחלקי {=במה שחלקתי} המעשיות והדרשות לחלקיהן, ובהביאי דמיון כל חלק וחלק, כי פרשתי {על ידי} זה כל הדרשות והמעשיות שנמצאים בתלמוד בכח הקרוב למי שמבין, כי ידעתי כי לא יקשה אחרי זאת על המבין, כשיראה דרש או מעשה שישמענו שידע ויבין מאיזה חלק הוא מהחלקים שזכרנו.

ובזה ימלט נפשו מלהוציא על המדברים ז"ל דבות שלא כראוי - כאשר יוציאו הקראים והכסילים וכיוצא בהם. או {ימלט נפשו} ש{לא} יטבע ביון הסכלות בדברים הנמנעים, ויחשוב שימצא דבר שאינו מצוי (ושאירע) [ושיארע] דבר שלא היה

One [who believes such matters may] deny [the essence of] God, may He be blessed, by assigning Him physical properties or the like. Such would happen if one were to explain these exegeses according to their simple explanation and believe them accordingly,[1] as the Sages stated: "The student who strays, his master he blames."[2, 3]

Contemplate this principle, for it is a great pillar and a fortified wall, which I have explained with the help of my God and His assistance. He opened the gates of understanding for me, and assisted me with what I explained in this book. Now, you are blessed by God.[4] Place me as a seal upon your heart,[5] and as a symbol between your eyes.[6]

Let this serve you as a prelude and introduction for all that you read or hear of exegeses or narratives, and it shall benefit you greatly. You

---

the Sages, of blessed memory, such that when the other nations hear them, they say, "This is certainly a foolish and villainous people, this small nation."

1 RaAVa"D critiques HaRaMBa"M's insistence that one who believes in the corporeality of God is a heretic (*Hilkhot Teshuva* 3:7):

> Why does he (HaRaMBa"M) call such a person a heretic? For many who were greater and better than him subscribed to this thought in accordance with what they saw in Scripture, and even more so because of what they saw in the *aggadot*, which distorted [their] thinking.

2 The source of this idiom is unclear.

3 This is similar to what HaRaMBa"M writes (*Guide*, II, 47):

> You must explain passages not quoted by me by those which I have quoted in this chapter. Employ your reason, and you will be able to discern what is said allegorically, figuratively, or hyperbolically, and what is meant literally, exactly according to the original meaning of the words. You will then understand all prophecies, learn and retain rational principles of faith, pleasing in the eyes of God Who is most pleased with truth, and most displeased with falsehood; your mind and heart will not be so perplexed as to believe or accept as law that which is untrue or improbable, whilst the Law is perfectly true when properly understood. Thus Scripture states, "Thy testimonies are righteousness for ever" (Psalms 119:144); and "I the Lord speak righteousness" (Isaiah 45:19). If you adopt this method, you will not imagine the existence of things which God has not created, or accept adverse principles which may lead to heresy, or to a corruption of your notions of God so as to ascribe to Him corporeality, attributes, or emotions, as has been shown by us. Nor will you believe that the words of the Prophets are false: for the cause of this disease is ignorance of what we have explained. These things belong likewise to the mysteries of the Law; and although we have treated them in a general manner, they can easily be understood in all their details in accordance with the above remarks.

4 based on Genesis 26:29

5 based on Song of Songs 8:6

6 based on Exodus 13:16

ונברא. ו{ימלט נפשו שלא} **יבוא לכפור בהשי"ת בהגשימו אותו וכיוצא בזה,** ו{אמנם} **כן יקרהו** בפרשו אותם הדרשות על פי פשטן והאמינו אותם על דרך ההיא - כמו שאמרו חז"ל **תלמיד תועה ברבו תולה.**

והתבונן עיקר זה כי הוא עמוד גדול וחומה בצורה, ביארתי בסיוע אלי ובעזרתו שפתח לי שערי בינה ועזרני מה שביארתי בספר הזה. ועתה אתה ברוך ה' שימני כחותם על לבך,[סג] וכטוטפות בין עיניך.[סד]

יהיה לך לפתח והקדמה לכל אשר תקרא או תשמע מהדרשות והמעשיות, ויועילך תועלת גדולה. ותהיה

shall be of those who understand truth and discern it, not those who go after delusion and are deluded. May He, may He be exalted, in His mercy straighten our curves and align our steps to follow the paths of truth and to walk in His ways, may His name be blessed from now to eternity,[1] Amen.

◆◆◆

1 based on Psalms 113:2

ממשכילי האמת ומכיריו, ולא מהפכם ההולכים אחרי ההבל ויהבלו.[סי] והוא יתעלה ברחמיו יישר מעגלותינו ויכין צעדינו לדרוך בנתיבות האמת וללכת בארחותיו, יהי שמו מבורך מעתה ועד עולם אמן.

◆◆◆

הערות שוליים

א. ע"פ שמות לד:ל
ב. ע"פ שמות ד:טז
ג. שמות יד:כא
ד. מלכים ב ב:ח, יד
ה. ויקרא יט:טו
ו. דברים א:יז
ז. ע"פ מלכים א ה:יא
ח. דברים יז:יא
ט. חולין קכד.
י. שבת סו:
יא. שבת סז.
יב. ברכות סב:
יג. יבמות עו:, כריתות טו:
יד. ברכות ח. ועוד
טו. שבת מ. ועוד
טז. עדיות א:יב, יבמות קטז:
יז. בבא בתרא קכז., זבחים לד:, נדה סח.
יח. לד:
יט. לא.
כ. לא.
כא. ה.
כב. תהלים ד:ה
כג. דברים ו:ז
כד. במדבר טו:לט
כה. שם פס' מ-מא
כו. אבות ג:א
כז. ח:
כח. ט.
כט. מלאכי ג:י
ל. מכילתא פר' יתרו, זבחים קטז.
לא. שמות יח:א
לב. שם
לג. שם
לד. מכילתא פר' בשלח
לה. שמות יד:טו
לו. ג.
לז. סב:
לח. דברי הימים א ח:לח
לט. שם ט:מד
מ. ב:ו, כח.
מא. לד:
מב. ל:-לא.
מג. ג:ח, יט.
מד. דברים ד:ז
מה. ישעיה נח:ט
מו. תהלים לא:טו
מז. יט:-כ.
מח. פג:
מט. ז.
נ. ז.
נא. כט.
נב. ז:
נג. ישעיה לח:ט
נד. כתובות ו.
נה. סב:
נו. נג.
נז. שמואל ב כג:כ, דהי"א יא:כב
נח. שם
נט. יח.
ס. סג.
סא. יד:
סב. חגיגה שם
סג. ע"פ שה"ש ח:ו
סד. ע"פ שמות יג:טז
סה. ע"פ מלכים ב יז:טו, ירמיה ב:ה

Contributors

ABOUT THE TRANSLATOR AND ANNOTATOR

Born and raised in South Florida, Rabbi Yitzhak Berdugo studied at Yeshivat Beth Moshe Chaim (Talmudic University) in Miami Beach and recieved his *semikha* under the auspices of its *Rosh Yeshiva*, Rabbi Yochanan Moshe Zweig, *SHeLIṬ"A*. While further studying in New York, Rabbi Berdugo received his *Yoreh Yoreh* from Rabbi Eliyahu Ben Haim, *Rosh Yeshiva* and *Av Bet Din* of *BaDa"Ṣ* Mekor Haim, Queens, New York, followed by a *Qabalah* in *sheḥiṭa* and in lung-checking.

Following in the path of the illustrious *Rabbanim* of the Berdugo family, Rabbi Berdugo has written much on *Halakha* and has authored his own responsa covering a variety of topics. With a great admiration for the *Ḥakhamim* of Sepharad, Rabbi Berdugo has a passion in the translation and and promulgation of their works.

Currently residing in Miami Beach, Florida, Rabbi Berdugo serves as the *Rosh Kollel* of the Bal Harbour Kollel and is pursuing his *Dayanut* qualification through the Eretz Hemdah Institute of Jerusalem and Montefiore Endowment.

ABOUT THE EDITORS

Avner Yeshurun, 22, was born in Israel and was raised in the sunny Caribbean island of Curaçao. He studied at the Hebron Yeshiva in Jerusalem. He is currently studying finance, fintech, accounting, and art history and technique at the University of Miami. When he isn't busy with homework – or research and publication for The Ḥabura – he can be found building his Jewish research library or spending time with local Ḥabura members. He enjoys translating notable pieces of research in the field of Jewish studies, and has a particular passion for translation and Jewish history. He hopes to publish his own research in the coming years through the Ḥabura. Though his heart is in the East, he is at the end of the West in Miami Beach, with his wife Elisheva and son Ariel Moshe.

Nachman Davies is an Israeli author, born on Merseyside in the early 1950s. His writings are concerned with Jewish spirituality and contemplative prayer, and he has spent many years living as a solitary Jewish Contemplative. He made *ạliyah* (from Spain) in 2019 and now lives in Safed. His website is https://jewishcontemplatives.blogspot.com.

◆◆◆

דפוס דעת

DA'AT PRESS

About Da'at Press

Da'at Press is dedicated to publishing works by Jewish scholars of the past, present, and future.

To find out more about our books and online learning community, please visit www.daat.press

◆◆◆

Printed in Great Britain
by Amazon

26244362R00101